Vegan Air Fryer Cookbook for Beginners

1000-Day Delicious, Healthy Plant-Based Recipes to Enjoy Deep-Fried Flavors

Migan Barkey

© Copyright 2021 Migan Barkey - All Rights Reserved.

In no way is it legal to reproduce, duplicate, or transmit any part of this document by either electronic means or in printed format. Recording of this publication is strictly prohibited, and any storage of this material is not allowed unless with written permission from the publisher. All rights reserved.

The information provided herein is stated to be truthful and consistent, in that any liability, regarding inattention or otherwise, by any usage or abuse of any policies, processes, or directions contained within is the solitary and complete responsibility of the recipient reader. Under no circumstances will any legal liability or blame be held against the publisher for any reparation, damages, or monetary loss due to the information herein, either directly or indirectly.
Respective authors own all copyrights not held by the publisher.

Legal Notice:

This book is copyright protected. This is only for personal use. You cannot amend, distribute, sell, use, quote or paraphrase any part of the content within this book without the consent of the author or copyright owner. Legal action will be pursued if this is breached.

Disclaimer Notice:

Please note the information contained within this document is for educational and entertainment purposes only. Every attempt has been made to provide accurate, up-to-date and reliable, complete information. No warranties of any kind are expressed or implied. Readers acknowledge that the author is not engaging in the rendering of legal, financial, medical or professional advice.

By reading this document, the reader agrees that under no circumstances are we responsible for any losses, direct or indirect, which are incurred as a result of the use of information contained within this document, including, but not limited to, errors, omissions, or inaccuracies.

Table of contents

Introduction 6
Chapter 1: Vegan Basics 7
Chapter 2: Air Fryer Basics 11
Chapter 3: 21-Day Meal Plan to Start Your Journey 15
Chapter 4: Breakfast and Brunch Recipes 18

    Eggplant Bacon 18
    Tofu and Potato Scramble 19
    Balsamic Tofu Bacon 20
    French Toast 21
    Falafel 22
    Breakfast Frittata 23
    Tofu & "Sausage" Sandwich 24
    Loaded Hash Browns 25
    Breakfast Sandwich 26
    Breakfast Potatoes 27
    "Bacon" Breakfast 28
    Breakfast Casserole 29
    Omelets 30
    Breakfast Sandwich 31
    Breakfast Tofu Scramble 33
    Broccoli 34
    Breakfast Potatoes 35
    French Toast 36
    Breakfast Burrito 37
    Fruit Crumble 38

Chapter 5: Appetizer and Snack Recipes 39

    Baked Potatoes 39
    Kale Chips 40
    Avocado Fries 41
    Buffalo Cauliflower Wings 42
    Roasted Almonds 43
    Popcorn Tofu 44
    Fried Ravioli 45
    Onion Appetizers 46
    Avocado Rolls 47
    Spiced Chickpeas 48
    Black Bean Burger 49
    Fried Ravioli 50
    Zucchini Chips 51
    Corn Fritters 52
    Sweet Potato Tots 53
    Croutons 54
    Mushroom Pizza 55
    Sweet Potato Tots 56
    Veggie Wontons 57
    Crispy Brussels Sprouts 58

Chapter 6: Main Dish Recipes 59

    Cauliflower and Broccoli Bites 59
    Parmesan Eggplant with Pasta 60
    Thai Style Crab Cakes 62
    Pineapple and Tofu Kabobs 63
    Jackfruit Taquitos 64
    Tofu and Cauliflower Rice 65
    Tofu Buddha Bowl 66
    Cauliflower Stir-Fry 67
    Sweet Potatoes and Brussels sprouts Bowls 68
    Mushroom Pizzas 69
    Green Bean and Mushroom Casserole 70
    Black Bean Burger 71
    Falafel 72
    Lentil Balls with Rice 73
    Seitan Riblets 74
    Lasagna 75
    Italian Tofu 76
    Eggplant Parmesan 77
    Buffalo Cauliflower 78
    Lemon Tofu 79
    Tofu Buddha Bowl 80
    Chickpea Tacos 81
    Fish Taco Wraps 82

Tempeh Kabobs 83
Barbecue Soy Curls 85
Cauliflower and Chickpea Tacos 86
"Crab" Cake 87
Sweet & Spicy Cauliflower 88
Mushroom & Green Bean Casserole .. 89
Cauliflower Steak............................ 90

Chapter 7: Vegetable and Sides Recipes 91

Maple Roasted Brussels sprouts 91
Roasted Butternut Squash with Mushrooms and Cranberries............... 92
Corn and Zucchini Fritters 93
Roasted Corn 94
Roasted Green Beans 95
Shishito Peppers.............................. 96
Cheesy Potatoes............................... 97
Roasted Garlic................................. 98
Kale Chips..................................... 99
Baby Bok Choy 100
Plantain Chips 101
Popcorn Tofu................................ 102
Crispy Vegetables 103
Baked Potatoes with Broccoli & Cheese 104
Roasted Spicy Carrots 105
Avocado Fries 106
Baked Tofu Strips........................... 107
Baked Artichoke Fries..................... 108
Spicy Sweet Potato Fries.................. 109
French Fries 110
Rosemary Potatoes 111
Crispy Zucchini Wedges 112
Sweet Potato Chips 113
Garlic Mushrooms 114

Chapter 8: Salad Recipes.. 115

Roasted Butternut Squash Salad 115
Garlic and Lemon Mushroom Salad .. 116
Taco Salad Bowl 117
Sweet Potato Croutons Salad............ 118
Brussel sprouts Salad...................... 119
Roasted Vegetable and Pasta Salad 120
Crispy Tofu & Avocado Salad 121
Vegetable & Pasta Salad.................. 122
Rainbow Vegetables Salad................ 123
Salad Topped with Garlic Croutons .. 124
Green Bean Salad........................... 125
Italian Tofu Salad........................... 126
Salad with Roasted Tomatoes 127
Vegetable Salad with Chimichurri Vinaigrette.................................. 128
Fried Chickpea Salad 130
Radish & Mozzarella Salad............... 131
Mixed Greens with Corn 132
Roasted Vegetable Salad 133
Roasted Butternut Squash Salad 134
Green Salad with Roasted Bell Peppers 135

Chapter 9: Dessert Recipes 136

Carrot Cake.................................. 136
Donuts.. 137
Cinnamon Churros 138
Apple and Blueberries Crumble 140
Baked Apples................................ 141
Stuffed and Spiced Baked Apples...... 142
Vegan Brownies............................. 143
Roasted Bananas 144
Fruit Kebab 145
Pear Crisp 146
Sweetened Plantains 147
Peanut Butter Balls 148
Brownies..................................... 149
Apple Chips 150
Sweet Potato Dessert Fries 151
Mug Carrot Cake 152
Donut Holes 153
Fruit Crumble 154
Baked Apples with Pumpkin Spice.... 155
Berry Crumble 156

Conclusion 157

Introduction

Do you feel like making a significant lifestyle change? Are you willing to improve your life and to start looking and feeling awesome? Then you are probably in the best place! We are about to show you that you can become a new person in no time just by making some small but very important changes! So, here we go!

The first change you need to make regards your dietary habits! Therefore, you need to forget about the meals you are used to eating! You need to focus on adopting a new diet and we think that the best one for you would be the vegan one! Don't be afraid! This diet might seem to be pretty hard to follow but in fact, it's rather simple! Veganism just means you have to exclude the consumption of all kinds of animal products. You will have to exclude dairy products, eggs, honey and meat. Instead, you get to eat a lot of veggies, legumes, grains and fruits.

This brings us to the second change you need to make in order to look and feel great! It's the way you cook your meals! You need to forget about greasy meals, about fat ingredients! If you decided to become a vegan, you should probably find a healthier way to cook your dishes!

We want to help you with this aspect as well and that's why we suggest you try to using an air fryer instead of your regular pan and pot. Air fryers cook your meals using rapid air technology. This means that you can air fryer, grill, bake everything in such a healthy way! You don't need to use a lot of oil or fat because you can count on the circulation of hot air to cook your meals!

So, what do you say? Are you willing to give veganism a chance? And if that's the case, are you willing to try cooking your vegan dishes in your amazing air fryer? If the answer is yes, then you should know you've made the best decision! So, let's get started! Discover the best air fried vegan dishes ever! Have fun!

Chapter 1: Vegan Basics

What is Vegan?

Contrary to popular belief, vegan is not simply a type of diet.
It is actually a lifestyle that involves abstinence from the use of any animal products, not just food but any other product made from animal-derived materials (e.g. bags made from crocodile skin, jackets made of bear's fur and so on).
In this book, we will focus primarily on vegan diet, which is often confused with vegetarian diet.
In a vegetarian diet, the dieter consumes primarily fruits and vegetables and completely avoids meat, fish, seafood and poultry. However, the difference between vegans and vegetarians is that the latter still consumes animal derived products that are non-meat such as eggs, honey, milk and dairy. Vegans do not consume anything that is made of or by animals.

Why We Eat Vegan

Vegans have various reasons for adopting this type of diet.
Many do for health reasons.
In a report by the Academy of Nutrition and Diabetics, it has been shown that vegans are at less risk of many serious health conditions including cancer, heart disease, diabetes and high blood pressure, among others.
Research has also proven that vegans on average weigh 20 pounds lighter than people who consume meat. But unlike weight loss fad diets, this one produces long-term results and does not leave you feeling sluggish and weak.
Other vegans do this to save animals. Going vegan actually helps save up to 200 animals each year. This not only reduces the number of deaths but also prevents major sufferings in animal farms. Choosing plant-based food products is definitely the way to go for many animal lovers.

Guidelines and Rules for Eating Vegan

There are actually different types of vegan diets that you have to know about, and right away, you'll get the guidelines and rules for each one. They are quite simple and straightforward.

- **Whole food vegan diet**

This vegan diet focuses on the consumption of whole plant foods including whole grains, legumes, nuts, seeds, fruits and vegetables.

- **Raw food vegan diet**

This one involves eating fruits and vegetables and other plant foods that are raw and fresh, or are cooked at temperatures below 118 degrees F.

- **80/10/10 vegan diet**

In this type of vegan diet, you will have to limit intake of plants that are rich in fat such as nuts, avocados, and so on. Instead, you will consume mainly fresh raw fruits and leafy greens.

- **Starch solution vegan diet**

This refers to a low-fat, high-carb vegan diet that focuses on consumption of cooked starches such as rice, corn and potatoes.

- **Junk food vegan diet**

In this type of diet, the person eats mock meats and mock cheeses, vegan desserts and other processed vegan foods.

It depends on you which one you should follow but basically, it would be a good idea to eat a balanced vegan diet. You can eat processed vegan foods occasionally but make sure that you also eat whole plant foods and fresh raw fruits.

What to Eat

Here's a list of the foods that you can eat:
- Fruits and vegetables
- Tofu, tempeh, seitan
- Legumes (beans, lentils, peas)

- Nuts and nut butters
- Seeds (hemp, chia, flaxseeds, sunflower seeds)
- Vegan milks and yogurts
- Nutritional yeast
- Whole grains, cereals
- Plant foods (miso, kimchi, pickles, kombucha)
- Mushrooms
- Non-dairy milk (almond milk, soy milk, coconut milk)

Basically, anything derived from plants can be consumed in a vegan diet as long as edible and healthy. You can also eat food products designed for vegan diet (vegan butter, vegan cheese, and so on).

What Not to Eat

Here's a list of foods that you cannot eat:
- Meat (beef, lamb, pork, organ meat, horse, veal)
- Poultry (chicken, turkey, duck, quail, goose)
- Fish and seafood
- Dairy (milk, yogurt, cheese, butter, cream, ice cream)
- Eggs
- Any bee product
- Any product with animal-based ingredients (egg whites, whey, lactose, casein, gelatin)

Remember, if the food product is from animal or created by animals, you cannot consume it if you're a vegan.

Tips for Success

Going vegan is not that easy. But here are tips on how you can achieve success with it:

Tip # 1 – Go slow

It may not be easy to suddenly shift to a meatless diet. Vegan is quite restrictive that you may find it difficult to adopt this diet at first. Don't worry. You can start gradually. You can start by first eliminating meat and meat products from your diet. Once you get used to it, then you can start avoiding other animal-derived products such as eggs, dairy and so on.

Tip # 2 – Don't succumb to pressures from people around you

People around you may not understand your decision to go vegan.

But you don't have to worry about what they think or what they say because this is your body, so it's ultimately your decision.

Also, you have to keep in mind that you're not doing anything bad, and that vegan diet is actually beneficial for your health.

Tip # 3 – Plan your meals

It helps to plan your meals by creating a weekly menu and listing down all the ingredients that you'll need to prepare these dishes.

Choose those that are easy and quick to prepare especially during times when you're busy so that you won't get tempted to go back to your old meat-eating ways.

Tip # 4 – Plan dining out

Eating at restaurants and at parties can be a challenge for any vegan.

Before going to a specific restaurant, check out if the menu has options for vegans. Go to restaurants that do have vegan menu selections.

If you are invited to a party, let your friend know that you have adopted a vegan lifestyle and that you will appreciate it if there are vegan foods that can be served for you.

Tip # 5 – Consider taking supplements

Going on a vegan diet may mean missing out on certain key nutrients that the body needs to thrive and be healthy. One example is vitamin B12.

Consider taking a supplement for this vitamin so that you do not end up becoming vitamin B12 deficient.

Be sure to consult your doctor first before taking any supplement.

Chapter 2: Air Fryer Basics

What Is an Air Fryer?

With great technology coming through the market day after day, one device has changed the way we see deep-fried foods. An Air Fryer is a kitchen device made for multi-purpose cooking. It can be used for many different functions such as grilling, frying, roasting, and baking. People often confuse this new appliance with stove pressure cookers, but they are two very different devices. An air fryer is a smaller device than a pressure cooker. It is also way easier to clean it because of its small size. A pressure cooker is mainly used to handle liquids and soups, while an Air Fryer is not designed for liquid use. Any item that requires any form deep or pan-frying, it is better done with an air fryer.

Air Fryer has a modern design that even makes it look portable. Its compact design also helps in cooking food quickly. It comprises a timer which is used to set the time of cooking of each food. It also has a temperature controller like an oven so that you have more control over the cooking process. Different types of food require different times and temperatures. It has a stainless-steel frying basket to put food in. It is recommended to keep checking the food every 20 minutes; the time will continue even if the frying basket is taken out. The temperature ranges from 175F to 400F.

Advantages of Using an Air Fryer

The Air Fryer is becoming more and more popular these days; everyone is talking about how to make your meals more oil-free and healthier. This device achieves so much that it is very difficult not to discuss it these days. Many of its advantages include:

- **Diversity**

It has a diverse set of uses from grilling, roasting frying, and so much more. It cuts down the need for buying more appliances because of its vast range of uses. It can cook many different types of foods as well from chips, chicken wings, or burgers. All of the items need a different time of cooking, but all are cooked efficiently with this device.

- **Oil-free**

People that areorie conscious or just looking for a way to reduce fat in their diet, Air Fryer is the device they can use. Its way of cooking by circulating heated air around the cooking basket with almost no use of oil makes the dishes healthier and lighter in

consumption.
- **Reheating food**

When reheating leftovers or cold delivery food, you want to preserve the taste and freshness as much as you can. The air fryer does the job perfectly.
- **Time management**

Everyone spends so much on fast food because it is convenient and saves them a lot of time. This often comes with the cost of one's health. With an air fryer, quick recipes can be made with ease without the usual compromise on health.
- **Reduce Kitchen injuries**

With no use of oil, a lot of injuries come down too. You might have been burnt by the sizzle of a hot oil many times, but this risk reduces to nil with the use of air fryer.

How Does It Work?

As new devices are produced, our daily lives have become more and more easy. Air Fryer has made use of modern technology to help us navigate the kitchen effortlessly.

An Air Fryer is a very user-friendly device that works like a miniature convection oven. It has a power turbo countertop convection oven, which is its main unit. It cooks food by using a convection mechanism where hot air is circulated inside the machine cooking the food inside with crispiness and evenness. Convection is a process of transferring heat between particles. Hot air because it is denser, goes down the machine, and the cooler air rises.

Its method of cooking is better than other convection ovens and is also faster because of its small size. The small size speeds up the process of convection significantly. It has an electric coil that is inside the lid and a fan situated on top of the machine. When it is turned on, the electric coil in the machine heats, to desired set temperature, the compact air around it. The fan rotates that hot air through the entire compartment. The frying basket containing the food receives the hot air constantly throughout the time that it has been set to. This makes the food cook evenly with its taste all intact. The intensity of heat gives it its crispiness with no use of oil at all.

How to Start Cooking in An Air Fryer?

Air Fryer is very easy to use the device, and even someone with no experience can operate it without a glitch.

1. Place the Air Fryer over a heat resistant surface such as a marble counter and make sure that it has some space behind for the air to flow out. Make sure to place it where it cannot be damaged.
2. Now open the lid and remove the frying basket, it can be greased by oil if required by a brush.
3. As Air Fryer is like a miniature oven, it also needs to be preheated before use.
4. Load the frying basket with the food that needs to be cooked. Do not fill the entire basket but leave a third of its portion empty so air can circulate.
5. Put the frying basket inside the machine, secure it tightly, and shut the lid.
6. Put the power port inside a socket and turn on the electricity, the indicators of time and temperature will light up, showing that it is turned on. Set the time and temperature based on what type of food you are preparing.
7. Constantly check the food every 15 to 20 min by shaking, stirring, or flipping the contents.
8. When the cooking process is finished, a beep will be heard, and the device will shut down automatically. Give it a minute to shut down fully.
9. Take out the food from the frying basket and serve it hot on a plate.
10. Set the fryer aside, and don't use it until the device cools down. Clean the device before using it again.

How to Clean and Maintain Your Air Fryer

It is recommended to clean the Air Fryer every month thoroughly. If you fail to do so, then the machine will start to accumulate filth and give off an unpleasant smell. Also, during the cooking process, it might release black smoke from behind. This is no cause for alarm, but it might affect the overall taste of your food. Unlike cooking like the old days, the Air Fryer only has a frying basket utensil that will need cleaning rather than an array of spoons and pans. The frying basket can become greasy over time with multiple uses, so its cleaning is vital. Here are the steps on how to clean your device

1. First, switch off the device, then put the electric cord neatly down, and wait till the device completely cools down.
2. Now, take off the lid and take out the frying basket. It might be greasy, and food particles may be stuck on the bottom. To remove them, put a lot of water in a large container and mix in dishwater soap. Leave the frying basket in the solution for 10 to 15 minutes.

3. Do not use abrasive cleaning techniques and equipment that can remove the stainless-steel coating of the basket.
4. Later, take it out and scrub it down with a sponge.
5. Pat the basket gently, dry it using a kitchen towel or a napkin. After it is perfectly dry, reinsert it into the machine.

Chapter 3: 21-Day Meal Plan to Start Your Journey

Day 1

Breakfast: Scrambled Vegan Eggs and Fruits

Lunch: Avocado Rolls

Dinner: Cauliflower Steak

Day 2

Breakfast: Breakfast Burrito

Lunch: Buffalo Cauliflower

Dinner: Lasagna

Day 3

Breakfast: Vegan Omelet and Avocado Slices

Lunch: Seitan Riblets

Dinner: Roasted Vegetable Salad

Day 4

Breakfast: Breakfast Vegan Smoothie

Lunch: Black Bean Burger

Dinner: "Crab" Cake

Day 5

Breakfast: Breakfast Burrito

Lunch: Fried Ravioli

Dinner: Sweet & Spicy Cauliflower

Day 6

Breakfast: French Toast

Lunch: Chickpea Tacos

Dinner: Italian Tofu

Day 7

Breakfast: "Bacon" Breakfast

Lunch: Lentil Balls with Rice

Dinner: Vegetable and Pasta Salad

Day 8

Breakfast: Breakfast Tofu Scramble

Lunch: Barbecue Soy Curls

Dinner: Buffalo Cauliflower

Day 9

Breakfast: Breakfast Burrito

Lunch: Falafel

Dinner: Roasted Vegetable Salad

Day 10

Breakfast: Breakfast Frittata

Lunch: Lemon Tofu

Dinner: Mushroom and Green Bean Casserole

Day 11

Breakfast: Fruit Crumble

Lunch: Roasted Vegetable Salad

Dinner: Tofu Buddha Bowl

Day 12

Breakfast: Strawberry Smoothie

Lunch: Crispy Vegetables

Dinner: Lentil Balls with Rice

Day 13

Breakfast: Breakfast Potatoes

Lunch: Eggplant Parmesan

Dinner: Roasted Spicy Carrots

Day 14

Breakfast: Oats, Almond Milk and Fruits

Lunch: Crispy Zucchini Wedges

Dinner: Barbecue Soy Curls

Day 15

Breakfast: Quinoa Topped With Berries

Lunch: Crispy Tofu and Avocado Salad

Dinner: Italian Tofu

Day 16

Breakfast: Tofu & "Sausage" Sandwich

Lunch: Eggplant Parmesan

Dinner: Vegetable and Pasta Salad

Day 17

Breakfast: Breakfast Casserole

Lunch: Lentil Balls with Rice

Dinner: Chickpea Tacos

Day 18

Breakfast: Vegan Pancakes

Lunch: Cauliflower Steak

Dinner: Salad with Roasted Tomatoes

Day 19

Breakfast: Breakfast Sandwich

Lunch: Tofu Buddha Bowl

Dinner: Lasagna

Day 20

Breakfast: Tofu & "Sausage" Sandwich

Lunch: Roasted Butternut Squash Salad

Dinner: Eggplant Parmesan

Day 21

Breakfast: Breakfast Casserole

Lunch: Crispy Tofu and Avocado Salad

Dinner: Crispy Zucchini Wedges

Chapter 4: Breakfast and Brunch Recipes

Eggplant Bacon

Preparation Time: 10 minutes; Cooking Time: 30 minutes; Servings: 4

Ingredients:

- 1 medium eggplant, destemmed
- 1 teaspoon lemon juice
- 1/2 teaspoon ground black pepper
- 1/2 teaspoon salt
- 1 teaspoon smoked paprika
- 1/2 teaspoon cumin
- 1 teaspoon maple syrup
- 2 tablespoons soy sauce
- 1/4 teaspoon Worcestershire sauce, vegan
- 1 tablespoon toasted sesame oil
- 1 tablespoon olive oil
- Olive oil spray

Method:

1. Switch on the air fryer, insert the fryer basket, then shut it with the lid, set the frying temperature 300 degrees F, and let it preheat for 5 minutes.
2. Meanwhile, prepare the eggplant and for this, cut it into quarters, and then slice it into 1/8-thick long strips like bacon.
3. Take a small bowl, add remaining ingredients in it, stir until combined, and then brush the mixture on both sides of eggplant strips.
4. Open the preheated fryer, place eggplant strips in it in a single layer, spray with olive oil, close the lid and cook for 15 minutes until golden brown and dried, turning and spraying with oil halfway.
5. When done, the air fryer will beep, then open the lid, transfer eggplant strips to a dish and cover with foil to keep them warm.
6. Cook remaining eggplant strips in the same manner and then serve straight away.

Nutrition Value:

- Calories: 99
- Fat: 7.2 g
- Carbs: 8.9 g
- Protein: 1.7 g
- Fiber: 4.3 g

Tofu and Potato Scramble

Preparation Time: 10 minutes; Cooking Time: 30 minutes; Servings: 3

Ingredients:
- 1 block of tofu, pressed, drained, cut into 1-inch pieces
- 4 cups broccoli florets
- 1/2 cup chopped white onion
- 4 medium potatoes, peeled, 1-inch cubed
- 1/2 teaspoon onion powder
- 1/2 teaspoon garlic powder
- 1 teaspoon turmeric
- 2 tablespoons soy sauce
- 2 tablespoons olive oil, divided

Method:
1. Take a medium bowl, add tofu pieces in it, add onion, sprinkle with onion powder, garlic powder, and turmeric, drizzle with 1 tablespoon oil and soy sauce, toss until coated, and let it marinate for 15 minutes.
2. Meanwhile, switch on the air fryer, insert the fryer basket, then shut it with the lid, set the frying temperature 400 degrees F, and let it preheat for 5 minutes.
3. In the meantime, place potatoes in a small bowl, drizzle with remaining oil and toss until well coated.
4. Open the preheated fryer, place potatoes in it, close the lid and cook for 15 minutes until golden brown and cooked, shaking halfway.
5. Then add tofu into the fryer, reserving the marinade, shut with lid, and continue cooking for 10 minutes at 370 degrees F until cooked, shaking halfway.
6. Meanwhile, add broccoli florets into the reserved marinade and toss until well coated.
7. When 10 minutes of frying time is up, add broccoli florets into the fryer, toss until mixed, shut with lid, and continue cooking for 5 minutes until cooked, shaking halfway.
8. When done, the air fryer will beep and then open the lid and transfer scramble to a dish.
9. Serve straight away.

Nutrition Value:
- Calories: 286
- Fat: 20.7 g
- Carbs: 10.3 g
- Protein: 19.4 g
- Fiber: 3.3 g

Balsamic Tofu Bacon

Preparation Time: 35 minutes; Cooking Time: 40 minutes; Servings: 4

Ingredients:
- 1 block of tofu, pressed, drained, sliced
- 1 teaspoon garlic powder
- 1/4 cup soy sauce
- 1 tablespoon maple syrup
- 1 tablespoon liquid smoke
- 3 tablespoons balsamic vinegar
- Olive oil spray

Method:
1. Prepare the marinade and for this, take a small bowl, add garlic powder and then stir in soy sauce, maple syrup, liquid smoke, and vinegar until combined.
2. Cut tofu into slices, place them in a shallow dish, pour in prepared marinade, toss until well coated, and then marinate in the refrigerator for 30 minutes.
3. When ready to cook, switch on the air fryer, insert the fryer basket, then shut it with the lid, set the frying temperature 400 degrees F, and let it preheat for 5 minutes.
4. Then open the preheated fryer, place tofu slices in it in a single layer, spray with olive oil, close the lid and cook for 20 minutes until golden brown and cooked, turning and spraying with oil halfway.
5. When done, the air fryer will beep and then open the lid, transfer tofu slices to a dish and cover with a foil to keep them warm.
6. Cook remaining tofu slices in the same manner and then serve straight away.

Nutrition Value:
- Calories: 372.9
- Fat: 27.7 g
- Carbs: 33.6 g
- Protein: 26 g
- Fiber: 4 g

French Toast

Preparation Time: 5 minutes; Cooking Time: 12 minutes; Servings: 4

Ingredients:
- 4 slices of bread, whole-grain
- ½ cup rolled oats
- ½ cup pecans
- 1 tablespoon ground flax seed
- ½ teaspoon ground cinnamon
- 1/3 cup almond milk
- Maple syrup for serving
- Olive oil spray

Method:
1. Switch on the air fryer, insert the fryer basket, then shut it with the lid, set the frying temperature 350 degrees F, and let it preheat for 5 minutes.
2. Meanwhile, prepare the topping and for this, place oats in a food processor, add flax seeds, pecans, and cinnamon it and pulse for 2 minutes until the mixture resembles breadcrumbs.
3. Tip the mixture in a shallow dish, take another shallow dish, and pour milk in it.
4. Add bread slices, one at a time, and then let them soak for 15 seconds until side, don't let it mushy.
5. Open the preheated fryer, place prepared bread slices in it in a single layer, spray with olive oil, close the lid and cook for 6 minutes until golden brown and cooked, turning and spraying with oil halfway.
6. When done, the air fryer will beep, then open the lid, transfer the toast to a dish, sprinkle the prepared topping on it, and cover with foil to keep it warm.
7. Prepare the remaining toast in the same manner, sprinkle with remaining topping, and serve straight away.

Nutrition Value:
- Calories: 102.2
- Fat: 3.4 g
- Carbs: 28.2 g
- Protein: 6.2 g
- Fiber: 3.6 g

Falafel

Preparation Time: 50 minutes; Cooking Time: 35 minutes; Servings: 12

Ingredients:
- 15-ounce cooked chickpeas
- 3/4 cup minced white onion
- 2 teaspoons minced garlic
- 1/3 cup chopped parsley
- 1/4 teaspoon ground black pepper
- 1/4 teaspoon sea salt
- 2 tablespoons sesame seeds
- 1/8 teaspoon ground cardamom
- 1/8 teaspoon ground coriander
- 1 1/2 teaspoon cumin
- 4 tablespoons almond flour
- Panko bread crumbs as needed for coating
- Olive oil spray

Method:
1. Take a food processor, place chickpeas in it, add the next nine ingredients, pulse for 2 minutes until a crumbly dough comes together, and then blend in flour, 1 tablespoon at a time until the dough comes together.
2. Transfer the dough to a large bowl, cover with a plastic wrap and freeze for 45 minutes until firm.
3. Then switch on the air fryer, insert the fryer basket, then shut it with the lid, set the frying temperature 375 degrees F, and let it preheat for 5 minutes.
4. Meanwhile, shape the falafel mixture into twelve patties and then dredge into bread crumbs.
5. Open the preheated fryer, place falafel in it in a single layer, spray with olive oil, close the lid and cook for 15 minutes until golden brown and cooked, turning and spraying with oil halfway.
6. When done, the air fryer will beep, then open the lid, transfer falafel to a dish and cover with foil to keep them warm.
7. Cook the remaining falafel in the same manner and then serve straight away.

Nutrition Value:
- Calories: 91
- Fat: 5.8 g
- Carbs: 8.1 g
- Protein: 2.2 g
- Fiber: 1.6 g

Breakfast Frittata

Preparation Time: 15 minutes; Cooking Time: 20 minutes; Servings: 2

Ingredients:

- Cooking spray
- ¼ lb. breakfast sausage, cooked and crumbled
- 4 vegan eggs
- ½ cup vegan cheese
- 2 tablespoons red bell pepper, diced
- 1 green onion, chopped

Method:

1. Spray oil on a small cake pan.
2. Preheat your air fryer to 360 degrees F.
3. Combine all the ingredients in a bowl.
4. Pour the mixture into the cake pan.
5. Cook in the air fryer for 20 minutes.

Nutritional Value:

- Calories: 380
- 694 mg
- Carbs: 3 g
- Fiber: 1 g
- Protein: 31.2 g

Tofu & "Sausage" Sandwich

Preparation Time: 2 minutes; Cooking Time: 13 minutes; Servings: 2

Ingredients:

- 2 vegan bagels, sliced in half
- 2 vegan breakfast sausages
- ½ teaspoon oil
- 4 thin slices tofu
- Salt and pepper to taste
- ¼ teaspoon nutritional yeast flakes, divided
- ¼ teaspoon granulated onion, divided
- 2 tablespoons vegan cream cheese

Method:

1. Toast the bagels in your toaster until golden.
2. Set aside.
3. Air fry the sausages at 400 degrees F for 10 minutes, flipping once halfway through.
4. In a pan over medium heat, add the oil.
5. Sprinkle salt, pepper, nutritional yeast flakes and onion on both sides.
6. Cook the tofu until golden on both sides.
7. Spread cream cheese on the bagel and top with the sausage and tofu.
8. Place the other bagel slice on top.

Nutritional Value:

- Calories: 472
- Fat: 11 g
- Carbs: 57 g
- Fiber: 3 g
- Protein: 22

Loaded Hash Browns

Preparation Time: 25 minutes; Cooking Time: 20 minutes; Servings: 4

Ingredients:
- 3 medium russet potatoes, peeled, grated
- 1/4 cup chopped red peppers
- 1/4 cup chopped white onions
- 1/4 cup chopped green peppers
- 1 teaspoon minced garlic
- ½ teaspoon ground black pepper
- 1 teaspoon paprika
- 2/3 teaspoon salt
- 2 teaspoons olive oil

Method:
1. Take a medium bowl, place grated potatoes in it, cover with chilled water, and let it soak for 20 minutes.
2. Then drain the potatoes, pat dry with paper towels, place them in a bowl and add all the spices and oil until stir until combined.
3. Switch on the air fryer, insert the baking basket, add potatoes, then shut it with the lid, set the frying temperature 400 degrees F, and cook for 10 minutes until golden brown and cooked, shaking halfway.
4. Then add onions and peppers, shake until mixed, shut the fryer with lid and continue cooking for 10 minutes until cooked.
5. When done, the air fryer will beep and then open the lid and transfer potatoes to a dish.
6. Serve straight away.

Nutrition Value:
- Calories: 200
- Fat: 6.5 g
- Carbs: 7 g
- Protein: 3.5 g
- Fiber: 1 g

Breakfast Sandwich

Preparation Time: 10 minutes; Cooking Time: 10 minutes; Servings: 4

Ingredients:

- ½ teaspoon turmeric
- 1 teaspoon garlic powder
- ¼ cup light soy sauce
- Paprika to taste
- 4 slices tofu, cut into rounds using cookie cutter
- 4 vegan English muffins, sliced in half
- 4 teaspoons vegan mayonnaise
- 1 avocado, sliced
- 4 slices vegan cheese
- 4 white onion rings
- 4 slices tomato

Method:

1. In a bowl, mix turmeric, garlic powder, soy sauce and paprika.
2. Marinate tofu rounds for 10 minutes.
3. Cook in the air fryer at 400 degrees F for 10 minutes, shaking once halfway through.
4. Spread the mayo on the muffin and put the avocado and cheese on top.
5. Put the tofu above the cheese.
6. Top with onion ring and tomato slice.
7. Place the other half of the muffin on top.

Nutritional Value:

- Calories: 226
- Fat: 7.6g
- Carbs: 30.6g
- Fiber: 4.2g
- Protein: 11.2g

Breakfast Potatoes

Preparation Time: 35 minutes; Cooking Time: 30 minutes; Servings: 4

Ingredients:
- 3 large potatoes, peeled, ½-inch cubed
- 1 small red pepper, diced
- 1 teaspoon onion powder
- 1 medium white onion, peeled, diced
- 1 teaspoon garlic powder
- 1 teaspoon paprika
- 2 teaspoons sea salt
- 2 tablespoons olive oil

Method:
1. Place potatoes in a large bowl, cover them with chilled water and let them soak for 30 minutes.
2. Meanwhile, take a small bowl, place all the seasonings in it and stir until mixed, set aside until required.
3. Switch on the air fryer, insert the fryer basket, then shut it with the lid, set the frying temperature 370 degrees F, and let it preheat for 5 minutes.
4. Then drain the soaked potatoes, pat dries them, place them in a large bowl, drizzle with oil and mix until coated.
5. Open the preheated fryer, place potatoes in it, close the lid and cook for 20 minutes until golden brown and cooked, shaking halfway.
6. When done, the air fryer will beep and then open the lid and transfer potatoes to a large bowl.
7. Add diced onion and red pepper, mix well and then stir in prepared seasoning mix until coated.
8. Transfer the potato mixture into the fryer basket, spray with olive oil, close the lid and cook for 10 minutes at 380 degrees F until cooked, shaking halfway.
9. Serve straight away.

Nutrition Value:
- Calories: 135
- Fat: 2 g
- Carbs: 27 g
- Protein: 4 g
- Fiber: 3 g

"Bacon" Breakfast

Preparation Time: 15 minutes; Cooking Time: 25 minutes; Servings: 2

Ingredients:

- 2 tablespoons tamari
- 1 tablespoon sesame oil, toasted
- 1 tablespoon olive oil
- 1 teaspoon maple syrup
- 1 teaspoon lemon juice
- 1 teaspoon paprika
- Salt and pepper to taste
- ¼ teaspoon vegan Worcestershire sauce
- ½ teaspoon cumin
- 1 medium eggplant, cut into long thin slices
- 2 tablespoons vegan mayonnaise
- 2 vegan muffins
- 4 tomato slices
- 4 cucumber slices

Method:

1. Preheat your air fryer to 300 degrees F.
2. In a bowl, mix the tamari, oils, maple syrup, lemon juice, paprika, salt, pepper, Worcestershire sauce and cumin.
3. Brush both sides of eggplant slice with the mixture.
4. Arrange the eggplant slices on a single layer on the air fryer pan.
5. Cook for 15 minutes or until brown.
6. Spread mayo on the muffin and put the "bacon" on top.
7. Top with the cucumber and tomato slices.

Nutritional Value:

- Calories: 99
- Fat: 7.2 g
- Carbs: 8.9 g
- Fiber: 4.3 g
- Protein: 1.7 g

Breakfast Casserole

Preparation Time: 10 minutes; Cooking Time: 20 minutes; Servings: 2

Ingredients:

- 1 teaspoon olive oil
- 1 onion, diced
- 1 teaspoon garlic, minced
- ½ cup bell pepper, diced
- ½ cup mushrooms, sliced
- 2 stalks celery, chopped
- 1 carrot, chopped
- Salt and pepper to taste
- ½ teaspoon dried oregano
- ½ teaspoon dried dill
- ½ teaspoon cumin
- 7 oz. tofu
- 2 tablespoons water
- 2 tablespoons soy yogurt
- 2 tablespoons nutritional yeast
- 1 tablespoon lemon juice
- ½ cup cooked quinoa

Method:

1. Pour the olive oil in a pan over medium heat.
2. Cook the onion and garlic for 2 minutes.
3. Add the bell pepper, mushroom, celery and carrot.
4. Season with the salt, pepper, oregano, dill and cumin.
5. Mix well and cook for 3 minutes.
6. In a food processor, put the rest of the ingredients except the quinoa.
7. Pulse until creamy.
8. Pour the mixture into the pan and add the quinoa.
9. Mix well.
10. Transfer the mixture to a baking dish that will fit inside an air fryer.
11. Cook at 350 degrees F for 15 minutes.
12. Let cool a little before serving.

Nutritional Value:

- Calories: 352
- Fat: 10.4g
- Carbs: 47.8g
- Fiber: 9.6g
- Protein: 21.5g

Omelets

Preparation Time: 10 minutes; Cooking Time: 21 minutes; Servings: 4

Ingredients:
- ½ block of tofu, pressed, drained
- ¼ cup chickpea flour
- 3 tablespoons chopped kale
- 3 tablespoons chopped spinach
- 3 tablespoons chopped dried mushrooms
- ¼ teaspoon garlic powder
- ¼ teaspoon onion powder
- ¼ teaspoon ground black pepper
- ¼ teaspoon salt
- ½ teaspoon turmeric powder
- ¼ teaspoon dried basil
- ½ teaspoon cumin powder
- 3 tablespoons nutritional yeast
- 1 tablespoon Braggs
- ½ cup grated vegan cheese
- 1 tablespoon water
- Olive oil spray

Method:
1. Take a food processor, place all the ingredients in it except for cheese and vegetables and pulse for 2 minutes until batter comes together.
2. Transfer the batter into a large bowl, add cheese and chopped vegetables and mix until combined.
3. Switch on the air fryer, insert the fryer basket, then shut it with the lid, set the frying temperature 370 degrees F, and let it preheat for 5 minutes.
4. Meanwhile, prepare the omelet and for this, place a piece of parchment paper on working space, place a desired shape cookie cutter on it, press one-sixth of the prepared batter in it, and then lift the cookie cutter.
5. Prepare five more omelets in the same manner on the parchment sheet.
6. Open the preheated fryer, place omelets in it in a single layer, spray with olive oil, close the lid and cook for 8 minutes until golden brown and cooked, turning and spraying with oil halfway.
7. When done, the air fryer will beep and then open the lid, transfer omelets to a dish and cover with a foil to keep them warm.
8. Cook remaining omelets in the same manner and then serve straight away.

Nutrition Value:
- Calories: 104.6
- Fat: 1.9 g
- Carbs: 10.2 g
- Protein: 11.3 g
- Fiber: 0.3 g

Breakfast Sandwich

Preparation Time: 10 minutes; Cooking Time: 10 minutes; Servings: 4

Ingredients:

For the Tofu:
- 1 block of tofu, pressed, drained, cut into four round slices
- 1 teaspoon garlic powder
- 1/8 teaspoon paprika
- 1/2 teaspoon ground turmeric
- 1/4 cup soy sauce
- Olive oil spray

For the Sandwich:
- 1 medium avocado, peeled, pitted, sliced
- 4 slices of white onion
- 4 slices of tomato
- 4 tablespoons vegan mayonnaise
- 4 slices of vegan cheese
- 4 English muffins, whole-grain

Method:
1. Take a shallow dish, place tofu slices in it, add remaining ingredients for the tofu in it, toss until well coated, then cover the dish and let it marinate for a minimum of 10 minutes.
2. Meanwhile, switch on the air fryer, insert the fryer basket, then shut it with the lid, set the frying temperature 400 degrees F, and let it preheat for 10 minutes.
3. Then open the preheated fryer, place tofu in it in a single layer, spray with olive oil, close the lid and cook for 10 minutes until golden brown and cooked, turning and spraying with oil halfway.
4. When done, the air fryer will beep and then open the lid and transfer tofu to a plate.
5. Prepare the sandwich and for this, cut each muffin into half, then spread 1 tablespoon of mayonnaise in the bottom of each muffin and top with a slice of avocado, cheese, onion, and tomato.
6. Place a tofu slice on the topping, cover with the top half of the muffin and serve straight away.

Nutrition Value:
- Calories: 380
- Fat: 14 g
- Carbs: 45 g
- Protein: 21 g

- Fiber: 17 g

Breakfast Tofu Scramble

Preparation Time: 5 minutes; Cooking Time: 30 minutes; Servings: 3

Ingredients:

- 1 teaspoon turmeric
- 2 tablespoons soy sauce
- ½ teaspoon onion powder
- ½ teaspoon garlic powder
- ½ cup onion, chopped
- 2 tablespoons olive oil, divided
- 1 block tofu, cubed
- 2 ½ cups potato, cubed

Method:

1. In a bowl, combine the turmeric, soy sauce, onion powder, garlic powder, onion and half of the olive oil.
2. Marinate the tofu cubes in the mixture for 10 minutes.
3. In another bowl, coat the potato cubes with the remaining olive oil.
4. Cook the potatoes in the air fryer at 400 degrees F for 15 minutes, shaking halfway through.
5. Add the tofu and cook at 370 degrees F for another 15 minutes.

Nutritional Value:

- Calories: 168
- Fat: 10.7g
- Carbs: 15.2g
- Fiber: 2.4g
- Protein: 4.8g

Broccoli

Preparation Time: 5 minutes; Cooking Time: 15 minutes; Servings: 2

Ingredients:
- 4 cups broccoli florets
- 2/3 teaspoon ground black pepper
- 1 ½ teaspoon salt
- 1 tablespoon nutritional yeast
- 2 tablespoons olive oil

Method:
1. Switch on the air fryer, insert the fryer basket, then shut it with the lid, set the frying temperature 370 degrees F, and let it preheat for 5 minutes.
2. Meanwhile, take a large bowl, place florets in it, add remaining ingredients and toss until well mixed.
3. Open the preheated fryer, place florets in it in a single layer, close the lid and cook for 5 minutes until golden brown and cooked, shaking, and spraying with oil halfway.
4. When done, the air fryer will beep, then open the lid, transfer broccoli to a dish and cover with foil to keep it warm.
5. Cook remaining broccoli florets in the same manner and then serve straight away.

Nutrition Value:
- Calories: 176
- Fat: 14 g
- Carbs: 7 g
- Protein: 3 g
- Fiber: 4 g

Breakfast Potatoes

Preparation Time: 5 minutes; Cooking Time: 25 minutes; Servings: 4

Ingredients:

- 2 potatoes, chopped
- 2 teaspoons olive oil
- Salt and pepper to taste
- 1 onion, chopped
- 1 bell pepper, chopped

Method:

1. Toss the potatoes in oil and season with salt and pepper.
2. Cook in the air fryer at 400 degrees F for 10 minutes, shaking once halfway through.
3. Add the onion and bell pepper.
4. Toss to mix and cook for 400 degrees for another 10 to 15 minutes.

Nutritional Value:

- Calories: 81
- Fat: 10 g
- Carbs: 17 g
- Fiber: 3 g
- Protein: 3 g

French Toast

Preparation Time: 5 minutes; Cooking Time: 6 minutes; Servings: 8

Ingredients:

- 1 cup pecans
- 2 tablespoons flaxseeds
- 1 teaspoon ground cinnamon
- 1 cup rolled oats
- ¾ cup almond milk
- 8 pieces whole grain vegan bread
- Maple syrup

Method:

1. Pulse pecans, flaxseeds, cinnamon and oats in the food processor until crumbly.
2. Transfer to a dish.
3. In another place, pour in the almond milk.
4. Soak each bread slice for 10 seconds in the almond milk.
5. Dredge with the pecan mixture.
6. Cook the bread in the air fryer at 350 degrees for 3 minutes.
7. Flip the bread and cook for an additional 3 minutes.
8. Drizzle maple syrup on top.

Nutritional Value:

- Calories: 308
- Fat: 27.6g
- Carbs: 14.4g
- Fiber: 4.8g
- Protein: 4.9g

Breakfast Burrito

Preparation Time: 20 minutes; Cooking Time: 8 minutes; Servings: 4

Ingredients:

- 2 tablespoons tamari
- 2 tablespoons cashew butter
- 1 tablespoon water
- 1 tablespoon liquid smoke
- 4 pieces rice paper
- 2 vegan eggs
- ¼ cup sweet potatoes, cubed and roasted
- 8 strips red pepper, roasted
- 6 spears fresh asparagus
- 1 cup kale

Method:

1. In a bowl, mix the tamari, butter, water and liquid smoke.
2. Arrange the rest of the ingredients on top of the rice paper sheets.
3. Roll and seal the ends.
4. Dip each burrito into the tamari mixture.
5. Cook in the air fryer at 350 degrees F for 8 minutes or until crispy.

Nutritional Value:

- Calories: 255
- Fat: 5.2g
- Carbs: 39.6g
- Fiber: 5.9g
- Protein: 10.2g

Fruit Crumble

Preparation Time: 15 minutes; Cooking Time: 15 minutes; Servings: 2

Ingredients:

- 1 apple, diced
- ¼ cup frozen strawberries
- ¼ cup frozen blueberries
- 2 tablespoons sugar
- ¼ cup brown rice flour
- 2 tablespoons vegan butter
- ½ teaspoon ground cinnamon

Method:

1. Preheat your air fryer to 350 degrees F for 5 minutes.
2. In a ramekin, combine the apple, strawberries and blueberries.
3. In a bowl, mix the rest of the ingredients.
4. Pour the mixture over the fruits and mix well.
5. Cook in the air fryer at 350 degrees F for 15 minutes.

Nutritional Value:

- Calories: 310
- Fat: 12 g
- Carbs: 50 g
- Fiber: 5 g
- Protein: 2 g

Chapter 5: Appetizer and Snack Recipes

Baked Potatoes

Preparation Time: 5 minutes; Cooking Time: 40 minutes; Servings: 4

Ingredients:
- 4 large baking potatoes
- 4 tablespoons chopped parsley
- 1 teaspoon garlic powder
- 2 teaspoons ground black pepper
- 2 teaspoons salt
- 2 tablespoons olive oil
- 4 tablespoons almond butter, divided

Method:
1. Switch on the air fryer, insert the fryer basket, then shut it with the lid, set the frying temperature 400 degrees F, and let it preheat for 5 minutes.
2. Meanwhile, brush potatoes with oil, then season with garlic powder, salt, and black pepper, and sprinkle with parsley.
3. Open the preheated fryer, place potatoes in it, close the lid and cook for 40 minutes until golden brown and cooked, turning and spraying with oil halfway.
4. When done, the air fryer will beep and then open the lid and transfer potatoes to a dish.
5. Open the potatoes by slicing them in half lengthwise, top each potato with 1 tablespoon of butter and serve.

Nutrition Value:
- Calories: 161
- Fat: 0.2 g
- Carbs: 37 g
- Protein: 4.3 g
- Fiber: 3.8 g

Kale Chips

Preparation Time: 5 minutes; Cooking Time: 5 minutes; Servings: 2

Ingredients:
- 4 cups kale leaves, stems removed
- 1/4 teaspoon salt
- 2 teaspoons ranch seasoning, vegan
- 1 tablespoon nutritional yeast
- 2 tablespoons olive oil

Method:
1. Switch on the air fryer, insert the fryer basket, then shut it with the lid, set the frying temperature 370 degrees F, and let it preheat for 5 minutes.
2. Meanwhile, take a medium bowl, add kale chips and remaining ingredients and toss until coated.
3. Open the preheated fryer, place kale in it, close the lid and cook for 5 minutes until golden brown and cooked, shaking halfway.
4. When done, the air fryer will beep and then open the lid and transfer kale chips to a dish.
5. Serve straight away.

Nutrition Value:
- Calories: 98
- Fat: 4 g
- Carbs: 15.7 g
- Protein: 0 g
- Fiber: 2.7 g

Avocado Fries

Preparation Time: 5 minutes; Cooking Time: 10 minutes; Servings: 4

Ingredients:
- 1 medium avocado, peeled, pitted, sliced
- 1/2 teaspoon salt
- 1/2 cup panko breadcrumbs
- ¼ cup chickpeas liquid
- Olive oil spray

Method:
1. Switch on the air fryer, insert the fryer basket, then shut it with the lid, set the frying temperature 390 degrees F, and let it preheat for 5 minutes.
2. Meanwhile, take a shallow bowl, place breadcrumbs in it, season with salt, and stir until combined.
3. Take another shallow bowl, pour in chickpeas liquid, dip avocado slices in it and then dredge into breadcrumbs mixture until coated.
4. Open the preheated fryer, place avocado slices in it in a single layer, spray with olive oil, close the lid and cook for 10 minutes until golden brown and cooked, shaking, and spraying with oil halfway.
5. When done, the air fryer will beep and then open the lid and transfer avocado fries to a dish.
6. Serve straight away.

Nutrition Value:
- Calories: 132
- Fat: 11.1 g
- Carbs: 6.6 g
- Protein: 4 g
- Fiber: 4 g

Buffalo Cauliflower Wings

Preparation Time: 10 minutes; Cooking Time: 40 minutes; Servings: 4

Ingredients:
- 1 large head cauliflower, cut into florets
- 1 teaspoon minced garlic
- 1/2 cup Frank red hot sauce
- 2 tablespoons almond butter
- 1 cup of soy milk
- Olive oil spray

For the Batter:
- 1 cup almond flour
- 1/4 teaspoon dried chipotle chili
- 1/4 teaspoon cayenne pepper
- 1 teaspoon granules of chicken bouillon, vegan
- 1/4 teaspoon paprika
- 1/4 teaspoon red chili powder

Method:
1. Switch on the air fryer, insert the fryer basket, then shut it with the lid, set the frying temperature 390 degrees F, and let it preheat for 5 minutes.
2. Meanwhile, prepare the batter and for this, take a large bowl, place all its ingredients in it and whisk until smooth batter comes together.
3. Then add cauliflower florets in it and toss until well coated.
4. Open the preheated fryer, place cauliflower florets in it in a single layer, close the lid and cook for 20 minutes until golden brown and cooked, turning and spraying with oil halfway.
5. Meanwhile, prepare the sauce and for this, take a small saucepan, place it over medium-high heat, add butter in it, stir in garlic and hot sauce, bring the mixture to boil and then simmer over medium heat until thickened, covering the pan.
6. When done, the air fryer will beep, then open the lid, transfer cauliflower florets to a large dish and cover with foil to keep them warm.
7. Cook remaining cauliflower florets, in the same manner, add them to the bowl, then pour prepared sauce over them and toss until well coated.
8. Serve straight away.

Nutrition Value:
- Calories: 129
- Fat: 1 g
- Carbs: 24 g
- Protein: 7 g
- Fiber: 4 g

Roasted Almonds

Preparation Time: 5 minutes; Cooking Time: 6 minutes; Servings: 8

Ingredients:
- 2 cups almonds
- 1 tablespoon garlic powder
- 1/4 teaspoon ground black pepper
- 1 teaspoon paprika
- 1 tablespoon soy sauce

Method:
1. Switch on the air fryer, insert the fryer basket, then shut it with the lid, set the frying temperature 320 degrees F, and let it preheat for 5 minutes.
2. Meanwhile, take a large bowl, add almonds in it, then add remaining ingredients and toss until mixed.
3. Open the preheated fryer, place almonds in it, close the lid and cook for 6 minutes until golden brown and cooked, shaking halfway.
4. When done, the air fryer will beep and then open the lid and transfer almonds to a dish.
5. Serve straight away.

Nutrition Value:
- Calories: 7.7
- Fat: 0.7 g
- Carbs: 0.3 g
- Protein: 0.3 g
- Fiber: 0.1 g

Popcorn Tofu

Preparation Time: 15 minutes; Cooking Time: 12 minutes; Servings: 4

Ingredients:
- ½ cup cornmeal
- ½ cup quinoa flour
- 1 tablespoon vegan bouillon
- 2 tablespoons nutritional yeast
- 1 teaspoon garlic powder
- 1 teaspoon onion powder
- 1 tablespoon mustard
- Salt and pepper to taste
- ¾ cup almond milk
- 1 ½ cups breadcrumbs
- 14 oz. tofu, sliced into small pieces
- ½ cup vegan mayo
- 2 tablespoons hot sauce

Method:
1. In the first bowl, mix the first 8 ingredients.
2. In the second bowl, pour the almond milk.
3. In the third bowl, add the breadcrumbs.
4. Dip each tofu slice into each of the bowls starting from the flour mixture, then the almond milk and finally in the breadcrumbs.
5. Cook in the air fryer at 350 degrees F for 12 minutes, shaking halfway through.
6. Mix the mayo and hot sauce and serve with tofu.

Nutritional Value:
- Calories: 261
- Fat: 5.5 g
- Carbs: 37.5 g
- Fiber: 4.8 g
- Protein: 16 g

Fried Ravioli

Preparation Time: 5 minutes; Cooking Time: 24 minutes; Servings: 4

Ingredients:
- 8 ounces frozen vegan ravioli, thawed
- 1 teaspoon garlic powder
- 1 teaspoon dried oregano
- ¼ teaspoon ground black pepper
- ¼ teaspoon salt
- 1 teaspoon dried basil
- 2 teaspoons nutritional yeast
- 1/2 cup panko bread crumbs
- 1/4 cup chickpeas liquid
- 1/2 cup marinara
- Olive oil spray

Method:
1. Switch on the air fryer, insert the fryer basket, then shut it with the lid, set the frying temperature 390 degrees F, and let it preheat for 5 minutes.
2. Meanwhile, place bread crumbs in a shallow dish, add nutritional yeast and all the herbs and spices and stir until mixed.
3. Take a bowl, pour in chickpeas liquid in it, then dip ravioli in it and dredge into bread crumbs mixture until evenly coated.
4. Open the preheated fryer, place ravioli in it in a single layer, spray with olive oil, close the lid and cook for 12 minutes until golden brown and cooked, turning and spraying with oil halfway.
5. When done, the air fryer will beep, then open the lid, transfer ravioli to a dish and cover with foil to keep them warm.
6. Cook remaining ravioli in the same manner and then serve straight away.

Nutrition Value:
- Calories: 150
- Fat: 2 g
- Carbs: 27 g
- Protein: 5 g
- Fiber: 2 g

Onion Appetizers

Preparation Time: 10 minutes; Cooking Time: 4 minutes; Servings: 4

Ingredients:
- 2 lb. onions, sliced into rings
- 2 vegan eggs
- 1 cup almond milk
- 2 cups flour
- 1 tablespoon paprika
- Salt and pepper to taste
- 1 teaspoon garlic powder
- 1 teaspoon cayenne pepper
- Cooking spray
- ¼ cup vegan mayo
- ¼ cup vegan sour cream
- 1 tablespoon ketchup

Method:
1. Combine the eggs and milk in one plate.
2. In another plate, mix the flour, paprika, salt, pepper, garlic powder and cayenne pepper.
3. Dip each onion into the egg mixture before coating with the flour mixture.
4. Spray with oil.
5. Air fryer at 350 degrees F for 4 minutes or until golden and crispy.
6. Serve with the dipping sauces.

Nutritional Value:
- Calories: 364
- Fat: 14.5g
- Carbs: 52.7g
- Fiber: 7.2g
- Protein: 8.1

Avocado Rolls

Preparation Time: 20 minutes; Cooking Time: 25 minutes; Servings: 5

Ingredients:

- 10 rice paper wrappers
- 3 avocados, sliced
- 1 tomato, diced
- Salt and pepper to taste
- 1 tablespoon olive oil
- 4 tablespoons sriracha
- 2 tablespoons sugar
- 1 tablespoon rice vinegar
- 1 tablespoon sesame oil

Method:

1. Mash avocados in a bowl.
2. Stir in the tomatoes, salt and pepper.
3. Mix well.
4. Arrange the rice paper wrappers.
5. Scoop mixture on top.
6. Roll and seal the edges with water.
7. Cook in the air fryer at 350 degrees F for 5 minutes.
8. Mix the rest of the ingredients.
9. Serve rolls with the sriracha dipping sauce.

Nutritional Value:

- Calories: 422
- Carbs: 38.7g
- Fiber: 8.8g
- Protein: 3.8g

Spiced Chickpeas

Preparation Time: 5 minutes; Cooking Time: 20 minutes; Servings: 4

Ingredients:
- 19 ounces cooked chickpeas
- 3/4 teaspoon salt
- 2 teaspoons tandoori spice blend
- 1 tablespoon olive oil

Method:
1. Switch on the air fryer, insert the fryer basket, then shut it with the lid, set the frying temperature 390 degrees F, and let it preheat for 5 minutes.
2. Meanwhile, take a large bowl, place chickpeas in it, add remaining ingredients and toss until mixed.
3. Open the preheated fryer, place half of the chickpeas in it, close the lid and cook for 10 minutes until golden brown and cooked, shaking halfway.
4. When done, the air fryer will beep, then open the lid, transfer chickpeas to a dish and cover with foil to keep them warm.
5. Cook the remaining half of the chickpeas in the same manner and serve straight away.

Nutrition Value:
- Calories: 140
- Fat: 5 g
- Carbs: 17 g
- Protein: 6 g
- Fiber: 4 g

Black Bean Burger

Preparation Time: 10 minutes; Cooking Time: 25 minutes; Servings: 6

Ingredients:

- 1 ¼ cup rolled oats
- 16 oz. black beans, rinsed and drained
- ¾ cup salsa
- 1 tablespoon soy sauce
- 1 ¼ teaspoons chili powder
- ¼ teaspoon chipotle chili powder
- ½ teaspoon garlic powder

Method:

1. Pulse the oats inside a food processor until powdery.
2. Add all the other ingredients and pulse until well blended.
3. Transfer to a bowl and refrigerate for 15 minutes.
4. Form into burger patties.
5. Cook in the air fryer at 375 degrees F for 15 minutes.

Nutritional Value:

- Calories: 158
- Fat: 2 g
- Carbs: 30 g
- Fiber: 9 g
- Protein: 8 g

Fried Ravioli

Preparation Time: 15 minutes; Cooking Time: 8 minutes; Servings: 4

Ingredients:
- ½ cup panko breadcrumbs
- Salt and pepper to taste
- 1 teaspoon garlic powder
- 1 teaspoon dried oregano
- 1 teaspoon dried basil
- 2 teaspoons nutritional yeast flakes
- ¼ cup aquafaba liquid
- 8 oz. frozen vegan ravioli
- Cooking spray
- ½ cup marinara sauce

Method:
1. Mix the breadcrumbs, salt, pepper, garlic powder, oregano, basil and nutritional yeast flakes on a plate.
2. In another bowl, pour the aquafaba liquid.
3. Dip each ravioli into the liquid and then coat with the breadcrumb mixture.
4. Put the ravioli in the air fryer.
5. Spray oil on the raviolis.
6. Cook at 390 degrees F for 6 minutes.
7. Flip each one and cook for another 2 minutes.
8. Serve with marinara sauce.

Nutritional Value:
- Calories: 154
- Fat: 3.8g
- Carbs: 18.4g
- Fiber: 1.5g
- Protein: 4.6g

Zucchini Chips

Preparation Time: 5 minutes; Cooking Time: 24 minutes; Servings: 4

Ingredients:
- 1/2 cup almond flour
- 1 large zucchini, ¼-inch thick sliced
- 1/2 teaspoon garlic powder
- 1 teaspoon onion powder
- 1/2 teaspoon salt
- 1 teaspoon Italian seasoning
- 1/4 cup nutritional yeast
- 1/4 cup almond milk, unsweetened
- Olive oil spray

Method:
1. Switch on the air fryer, insert the fryer basket, then shut it with the lid, set the frying temperature 390 degrees F, and let it preheat for 5 minutes.
2. Meanwhile, place zucchini slices in a bowl, drizzle with milk and toss until coated.
3. Then take a shallow dish, place flour in it along with remaining ingredients, stir until combined, and then dredge each zucchini slice in it until evenly coated.
4. Open the preheated fryer, place zucchini slices in it in a single layer, spray with olive oil, close the lid and cook for 12 minutes until golden brown and cooked, turning and spraying with oil halfway.
5. When done, the air fryer will beep, then open the lid, transfer zucchini chips to a dish and cover with foil to keep them warm.
6. Cook remaining zucchini chips in the same manner and serve.

Nutrition Value:
- Calories: 165
- Fat: 1.2 g
- Carbs: 6 g
- Protein: 1.6 g
- Fiber: 2.2 g

Corn Fritters

Preparation Time: 15 minutes; Cooking Time: 10 minutes; Servings: 4

Ingredients:

- ¼ cup ground cornmeal
- ¼ cup flour
- Salt and pepper to taste
- ½ teaspoon baking powder
- ¼ teaspoon garlic powder
- ¼ teaspoon onion powder
- ¼ teaspoon paprika
- ¼ cup parsley, chopped
- 1 cup corn kernels mixed with 3 tablespoons almond milk
- 2 cups fresh corn kernels
- 4 tablespoons vegan mayonnaise
- 2 teaspoons grainy mustard

Method:

1. Mix the cornmeal, flour, salt, pepper, baking powder, garlic powder, onion powder, paprika and parsley in a bowl.
2. Put the corn kernels with almond milk in a food processor.
3. Season with salt and pepper.
4. Pulse until well blended.
5. Add the corn kernels.
6. Transfer to a bowl and stir into the cornmeal mixture.
7. Pour a small amount of the batter in the air fryer pan.
8. Pour another a few centimeters away from the first fritter.
9. Cook in the air fryer at 350 degrees for 10 minutes or until golden.
10. Flip halfway through.
11. Serve with mayo mustard dip.

Nutritional Value:

- Calories: 135
- Fat: 4.6g
- Carbs: 22.5g
- Fiber: 2.5g
- Protein: 3.5g

Sweet Potato Tots

Preparation Time: 5 minutes; Cooking Time: 28 minutes; Servings: 25

Ingredients:
- 2 cups sweet potato puree
- 1/2 teaspoon ground cumin
- 1/2 teaspoon salt
- 1/2 teaspoon ground coriander
- 1/2 cup Panko breadcrumbs
- Olive oil spray

Method:
1. Switch on the air fryer, insert the fryer basket, then shut it with the lid, set the frying temperature 390 degrees F, and let it preheat for 5 minutes.
2. Meanwhile, take a large bowl, place all the ingredients in it, stir until well combined, and then shape the mixture into twenty-five tots, each about 1 tablespoon.
3. Open the preheated fryer, place sweet potato tots in it in a single layer, spray with olive oil, close the lid and cook for 14 minutes until golden brown and cooked, turning and spraying with oil halfway.
4. When done, the air fryer will beep, then open the lid, transfer tots to a dish and cover with foil to keep them warm.
5. Cook remaining tots in the same manner and then serve straight away.

Nutrition Value:
- Calories: 26
- Fat: 0.2 g
- Carbs: 6 g
- Protein: 0 g
- Fiber: 2 g

Croutons

Preparation Time: 5 minutes; Cooking Time: 10 minutes; Servings: 4

Ingredients:
- 2 cups cubed bread, whole-grain
- 1/2 teaspoon garlic powder
- 1/3 teaspoon salt
- 1/2 teaspoon dried basil
- 1/4 teaspoon ground black pepper
- 1/2 teaspoon dried oregano
- 2 teaspoons lemon juice
- 2 teaspoons olive oil

Method:
1. Switch on the air fryer, insert the fryer basket, then shut it with the lid, set the frying temperature 400 degrees F, and let it preheat for 5 minutes.
2. Meanwhile, take a large bowl, place bread cubes in it, drizzle with lemon juice and oil, then sprinkle with remaining ingredients and toss until coated.
3. Open the preheated fryer, place croutons in it in a single layer, spray with olive oil, close the lid and cook for 5 minutes until golden brown and cooked, turning and spraying with oil halfway.
4. When done, the air fryer will beep, then open the lid, transfer croutons to a dish and cover with foil to keep them warm.
5. Cook remaining croutons in the same manner and serve.

Nutrition Value:
- Calories: 30
- Fat: 1 g
- Carbs: 4 g
- Protein: 0 g
- Fiber: 1 g

Mushroom Pizza

Preparation Time: 15 minutes; Cooking Time: 10 minutes; Servings: 4

Ingredients:
- 4 large Portobello mushrooms, stems and gills removed
- 1 teaspoon balsamic vinegar
- Salt and pepper to taste
- 4 tablespoons vegan pasta sauce
- 1 clove garlic, minced
- 3 oz. zucchini, chopped
- 4 olives, sliced
- 2 tablespoons sweet red pepper, diced
- 1 teaspoon dried basil
- ½ cups hummus
- Fresh basil, minced

Method:
1. Coat the mushrooms with balsamic vinegar and season with salt and pepper.
2. Spread pasta sauce inside each mushroom.
3. Sprinkle with minced garlic.
4. Preheat your air fryer to 330 degrees F.
5. Cook mushrooms for 3 minutes.
6. Take the mushrooms out and top with zucchini, olives, and peppers.
7. Season with salt, pepper and basil.
8. Put them back to the air fryer and cook for another 3 minutes.
9. Serve mushroom pizza with hummus and fresh basil.

Nutritional Value:
- Calories: 70
- Fat: 1.56 g
- Carbs: 11 g
- Fiber: 3.4 g
- Protein: 4.3 g

Sweet Potato Tots

Preparation Time: 10 minutes; Cooking Time: 12 minutes; Servings: 10

Ingredients:

- 2 cups sweet potato puree
- ½ teaspoon salt
- ½ teaspoon cumin
- ½ teaspoon coriander
- ½ cup breadcrumbs
- Cooking spray
- Vegan mayo

Method:

1. Preheat your air fryer to 390 degrees F.
2. Combine all ingredients in a bowl.
3. Form into balls.
4. Arrange on the air fryer pan.
5. Spray with oil.
6. Cook for 6 minutes or until golden.
7. Serve with vegan mayo.

Nutritional Value:

- Calories: 77
- Fat: 0.8g
- Carbs: 15.9g
- Fiber: 1.1g
- Protein: 1.8g

Veggie Wontons

Preparation Time: 10 minutes; Cooking Time: 15 minutes; Servings: 10

Ingredients:

- Cooking spray
- ½ cup white onion, grated
- ½ cup mushrooms, chopped
- ½ cup carrot, grated
- ¾ cup red pepper, chopped
- ¾ cup cabbage, grated
- 1 tablespoons chili sauce
- 1 teaspoon garlic powder
- Salt and pepper to taste
- 30 vegan wonton wrappers
- Water

Method:

1. Spray oil in a pan.
2. Put the pan over medium heat and cook the onion, mushrooms, carrot, red pepper and cabbage until tender.
3. Stir in the chili sauce, garlic powder, salt and pepper.
4. Let it cool for a few minutes.
5. Add a scoop of the mixture on top of the wrappers.
6. Fold and seal the corners using water.
7. Cook in the air fryer at 320 degrees F for 7 minutes or until golden brown.

Nutritional Value:

- Calories: 290
- Fat: 1.5g
- Carbs: 58g
- Fiber: 2.3g
- Protein: 9.9g

Crispy Brussels Sprouts

Preparation Time: 5 minutes; Cooking Time: 1 minutes; Servings: 2

Ingredients:

- 2 cups Brussels sprouts, sliced
- 1 tablespoon olive oil
- 1 tablespoon balsamic vinegar
- Salt to taste

Method:

1. Toss all the ingredients in a bowl.
2. Cook in the air fryer at 400 degrees F for 10 minutes, shake once or twice during the cooking process.
3. Check to see if crispy enough.
4. If not, cook for another 5 minutes.

Nutritional Value:

- Calories: 100
- Fat: 7.3g
- Carbs: 8.1g
- Fiber: 3.3g
- Protein: 3g

Chapter 6: Main Dish Recipes

Cauliflower and Broccoli Bites

Preparation Time: 5 minutes; Cooking Time: 12 minutes; Servings: 4

Ingredients:
- 1 cup panko bread crumbs
- ¼ cup grated vegan parmesan cheese
- 1 tablespoon creole seasoning
- 2 cups cauliflower florets
- 2 cups broccoli florets
- ½ cup whole-wheat flour
- 2 flax eggs
- 1 tablespoon chopped parsley
- Marinara sauce as needed for serving

Method:
1. Switch on the air fryer, insert the fryer basket, spray it with olive oil, then shut it with the lid, set the frying temperature 400 degrees F, and let it preheat for 5 minutes.
2. Meanwhile, take a large bowl, add bread crumbs in it and stir in seasoning and cheese until mixed, set aside until required.
3. Place flax eggs in another bowl, and then place flour in a shallow dish.
4. Prepare florets and for this, dredge broccoli and cauliflower florets into the flour, then dip into the flax eggs and coat with bread crumbs mixture until coated.
5. Open the preheated fryer, place florets in it in a single layer, spray with olive oil, close the lid and cook for 6 minutes until golden brown and cooked, shaking, and spraying with oil halfway.
6. When done, the air fryer will beep, then open the lid, transfer florets to a dish, and cover with a foil to keep them warm.
7. Cook remaining florets, in the same manner, sprinkle with parsley and serve with marinara sauce.

Nutrition Value:
- Calories: 130
- Fat: 3.5 g
- Carbs: 20 g
- Protein: 8 g
- Fiber: 2 g

Parmesan Eggplant with Pasta

Preparation Time: 5 minutes; Cooking Time: 16 minutes; Servings: 4

Ingredients:
- 1/2 cup almond flour
- 1 large eggplant, destemmed, sliced
- 1/3 teaspoon garlic powder
- 1/3 teaspoon onion powder
- ¼ teaspoon ground black pepper
- 1/3 teaspoon salt
- 1/2 cup panko bread crumbs
- 1/2 cup almond milk, unsweetened
- 2 tablespoons vegan grated parmesan

For the Topping:
- 1/2 cup shredded vegan mozzarella cheese
- 1 cup marinara sauce and more as needed for serving
- 1/3 cup grated vegan parmesan cheese

For Serving:
- 12 ounces cooked whole-grain pasta
- 1/3 cup vegan grated parmesan cheese
- 3 tablespoons chopped parsley

Method:
1. Switch on the air fryer, insert the fryer basket, then shut it with the lid, set the frying temperature 400 degrees F, and let it preheat for 5 minutes.
2. Meanwhile, place bread crumbs in a shallow dish and stir in garlic powder, onion powder, black pepper, salt, and cheese until mixed.
3. Take another shallow dish, place flour in it, then take a bowl and pour milk in it.
4. Prepare eggplants and for this, coat each slice with flour, then dip into milk and dredge with bread crumbs mixture until coated on both sides.
5. Open the preheated fryer, place eggplant slices in it in a single layer, spray with olive oil, close the lid and cook for 15 minutes until golden brown and cooked, turning and spraying with oil halfway.
6. When done, the air fryer will beep, then open the lid, top with marinara sauce and both cheeses, shut with lid, and cook for 1 minute until cheese has melted.
7. When done, transfer eggplant slices to a dish, add cooked pasta, garnish with parsley and parmesan cheese and serve.

Nutrition Value:
- Calories: 449.9
- Fat: 10.3 g
- Carbs: 41.7 g
- Protein: 22.5 g
- Fiber: 12 g

Thai Style Crab Cakes

Preparation Time: 15 minutes; Cooking Time: 40 minutes; Servings: 8

Ingredients:
- ¾ cup artichoke hearts, chopped
- 4 cups cubed potatoes
- 7 ounces hearts of palm, grated
- 1 bunch green onions, diced
- 1½-inch piece of ginger
- 2/3 teaspoon ground black pepper
- 1 teaspoon salt
- 1 lime, zested, juiced
- 4 tablespoons Thai Red Curry Paste
- 1 tablespoon soy sauce
- 4 sheets of nori
- Olive oil spray

Method:
1. Place potato cubes to a medium pot, cover them with water, place it over medium-high heat and boil for 5 to 8 minutes until fork tender.
2. Meanwhile, cut nori sheet into pieces, add them into a food processor along with onion and ginger, then add curry paste, soy sauce, lime juice, and zest and pulse for 2 minutes until the smooth paste comes together, set aside until required.
3. When potatoes have boiled, drain them, cool them for 10 minutes, then place them in a large bowl, add the prepared paste and stir well until combined.
4. Add artichokes and hearts of palm, stir until mixed, and then shape the mixture into eight patties.
5. Switch on the air fryer, insert the fryer basket, then shut it with the lid, set the frying temperature 350 degrees F, and let it preheat for 5 minutes.
6. Open the preheated fryer, place patties in it in a single layer, spray with olive oil, close the lid and cook for 15 minutes until golden brown and cooked, turning and spraying with oil halfway.
7. When done, the air fryer will beep, then open the lid, transfer patties to a dish and cover with foil to keep them warm.
8. Cook remaining patties in the same manner and serve straight away.

Nutrition Value:
- Calories: 97
- Fat: 0.4 g
- Carbs: 20 g
- Protein: 4 g
- Fiber: 5 g

Pineapple and Tofu Kabobs

Preparation Time: 15 minutes; Cooking Time: 30 minutes; Servings: 4

Ingredients:
- 1 medium pineapple, cubed
- 1 block of tofu, firmed, pressed, drained
- 1 medium white onion, peeled, cut into large chunks
- 2 medium green bell peppers, cored, cut into large chunks
- Soaked wooden skewers

For the Marinade:
- 1/2 teaspoon ground ginger
- 1/2 teaspoon paprika
- 1/2 cup tamari
- 1/4 cup maple syrup
- 1/2 cup water

Method:
1. Prepare the marinade and for this, take a shallow dish, place all its ingredients in it and whisk until combined.
2. Cut tofu into cubes, then add them into the marinade, toss until coated, and let them stand for 10 minutes.
3. Then Switch on the air fryer, insert the fryer basket, then shut it with the lid, set the frying temperature 320 degrees F, and let it preheat for 5 minutes.
4. Meanwhile, prepare kabobs, and for this, thread tofu alternating with the vegetables in the skewers.
5. Open the preheated fryer, place prepared kabobs in it in a single layer, spray with olive oil, close the lid and cook for 15 minutes until golden brown on all sides and cooked through, shaking and spraying with oil halfway.
6. When done, the air fryer will beep, then open the lid, transfer kabobs to a dish and cover with foil to keep them warm.
7. Cook remaining kabobs in the same manner and serve straight away.

Nutrition Value:
- Calories: 630
- Fat: 21 g
- Carbs: 83 g
- Protein: 31 g
- Fiber: 5 g

Jackfruit Taquitos

Preparation Time: 10 minutes; Cooking Time: 11 minutes; Servings: 4

Ingredients:
- 4 whole-wheat tortillas, 6-inch
- 1 cup cooked red beans
- 14 ounces of jackfruit, packed in water, drained
- ¼ cup and 2 tablespoons water
- ½ cup pico de gallo
- Olive oil spray

Method:
1. Switch on the instant pot, place jackfruit and beans in the inner pot, stir in pico de gallo sauce, pour in water, and shut with lid.
2. Then press the manual button and cook for 3 minutes at a low-pressure setting and, when done, release pressure naturally.
3. Open the lid, mash the jackfruit mixture, and set aside until required.
4. Switch on the air fryer, insert the fryer basket, then shut it with the lid, set the frying temperature 370 degrees F, and let it preheat for 5 minutes.
5. Meanwhile, prepare tortillas and for this, place ¼ cup of the bean-jackfruit mixture onto each tortilla and roll it up tightly, and prepare remaining tortillas in the same manner.
6. Open the preheated fryer, place tortillas in it in a single layer, spray with olive oil, close the lid and cook for 8 minutes until golden brown and cooked.
7. When done, the air fryer will beep and then open the lid and transfer tortillas to a dish.
8. Serve straight away.

Nutrition Value:
- Calories: 230
- Fat: 7.3 g
- Carbs: 38 g
- Protein: 4.6 g
- Fiber: 3 g

Tofu and Cauliflower Rice

Preparation Time: 5 minutes; Cooking Time: 22 minutes; Servings: 4

Ingredients:

For the Tofu:
- 1/2 block of tofu, extra-firm, pressed, drained
- 1 cup diced carrot
- 1/2 cup diced white onion
- 2 tablespoons soy sauce
- 1 teaspoon turmeric powder

For the Cauliflower Rice:
- 1/2 cup chopped broccoli
- 3 cups riced cauliflower
- 1 tablespoon minced ginger
- 1 teaspoon minced garlic
- 1/2 cup frozen peas
- 1 tablespoon apple cider vinegar
- 2 tablespoons soy sauce
- 1 1/2 teaspoons sesame oil
- Olive oil spray

Method:
1. Switch on the air fryer, insert the fryer baking pan, then shut it with the lid, set the frying temperature 370 degrees F, and let it preheat for 5 minutes.
2. Open the preheated fryer, add all the ingredients for the tofu in it, shake well until mixed, spray with olive oil, close the lid and cook for 10 minutes, shaking halfway.
3. Meanwhile, take a large bowl, place all the ingredients for cauliflower rice in it, and stir until combined.
4. When done, the air fryer will beep, open the lid, add cauliflower rice mixture, shake well to mix, and continue cooking for 12 minutes until cooked.
5. Serve straight away.

Nutrition Value:
- Calories: 86.9
- Fat: 0.6 g
- Carbs: 16.8 g
- Protein: 4.6 g
- Fiber: 5 g

Tofu Buddha Bowl

Preparation Time: 10 minutes; Cooking Time: 25 minutes; Servings: 6

Ingredients:
- 8 ounces spinach, sautéed with garlic in olive oil
- 2 cups cooked quinoa
- 3 medium carrots, peeled, sliced
- 14 ounces tofu, extra-firm, cut into small cubes
- 1 pound broccoli florets
- 1 medium red bell pepper, cored, sliced
- 3 tablespoons molasses
- 1/4 cup soy sauce
- 1 tablespoon Sriracha sauce
- 2 tablespoons lime juice
- 2 tablespoons sesame oil
- Olive oil spray

Method:
1. Prepare the marinade and for this, take a large bowl, add lime juice in it, whisk in molasses, Sriracha sauce, soy sauce, and sesame oil until combined, add tofu pieces in it, toss until well coated and marinate for 10 minutes, stirring occasionally.
2. Then switch on the air fryer, insert the fryer basket, spray with oil, then shut it with the lid, set the frying temperature 370 degrees F, and let it preheat for 5 minutes.
3. Open the preheated fryer, place tofu in it, close the lid and cook for 15 minutes until golden brown and cooked, shaking every 5 minutes.
4. Meanwhile, place all the vegetables into the marinade, except for spinach, toss until mixed and set aside until required.
5. When done, the air fryer will beep, open the lid, transfer tofu to a dish, add marinated vegetables in the fryer basket, shut with lid, and cook for 10 minutes, shaking halfway.
6. When done, assemble the bowl and for this, place quinoa in a large bowl, top with vegetables, spinach, and tofu in the ends, sprinkle with sesame seeds, drizzle with remaining marinade and serve.

Nutrition Value:
- Calories: 236
- Fat: 8 g
- Carbs: 31 g
- Protein: 12 g
- Fiber: 6 g

Cauliflower Stir-Fry

Preparation Time: 5 minutes; Cooking Time: 30 minutes; Servings: 4

Ingredients:
- 3/4 cup of onion white, peeled, sliced
- 1 large head of cauliflower, cut into florets
- 2 teaspoons minced garlic
- 1/2 teaspoon coconut sugar
- 1 tablespoon rice vinegar
- 1 1/2 tablespoons tamari
- 1 tablespoon Sriracha sauce
- 2 scallions, chopped
- Olive oil spray

Method:
1. Switch on the air fryer, insert the fryer baking pan, then shut it with the lid, set the frying temperature 350 degrees F, and let it preheat for 5 minutes.
2. Then add cauliflower florets, spray with olive oil, close the lid and cook for 10 minutes until golden brown, shaking halfway.
3. When done, the air fryer will beep, open the lid, add onion, stir until mixed, continue cooking for 10 minutes, then add garlic, stir until mixed, cook for 5 minutes.
4. Meanwhile, prepare the sauce and for this, place remaining ingredients in a small bowl and whisk until combined.
5. When vegetables have cooked, pour prepared sauce over them, toss until coated, and cook for another 5 minutes.
6. When done, transfer vegetables to a dish, sprinkle with scallions, and serve.

Nutrition Value:
- Calories: 93
- Fat: 3 g
- Carbs: 12 g
- Protein: 4 g
- Fiber: 3 g

Sweet Potatoes and Brussels sprouts Bowls

Preparation Time: 10 minutes; Cooking Time: 25 minutes; Servings: 4

Ingredients:
- 2 cups cooked quinoa
- 1/3 cup Tahini Dressing
- 1/3 cup peanut butter sauce
- 1/4 cup chopped green onion

For the Veggies:
- 4 cups sliced Brussels sprouts
- 6 cups diced sweet potato
- 2 teaspoons garlic powder, divided
- 2 tablespoons soy sauce

Method:
1. Switch on the air fryer, insert the fryer basket, then shut it with the lid, set the frying temperature 400 degrees F, and let it preheat for 5 minutes.
2. Then open the preheated fryer, place sweet potatoes in it, spray with olive oil, sprinkle with 1 teaspoon of garlic powder, shake well, close the lid and cook for 15 minutes until golden brown, shaking halfway.
3. When done, the air fryer will beep, open the lid, add sprouts, spray with oil, and sprinkle with remaining garlic powder, shake well to mix, close the lid and cook for 5 minutes until tender.
4. When done, drizzle soy sauce over vegetables, shake until mixed, shut with lid and continue cooking for 5 minutes until cooked and browned, shaking halfway.
5. Assemble the bowls and for this, divide quinoa between four bowls, top with vegetables, drizzle with peanut butter sauce and tahini dressing and sprinkle with green onion.
6. Serve straight away.

Nutrition Value:
- Calories: 357
- Fat: 26.1 g
- Carbs: 28.4 g
- Protein: 8.9 g
- Fiber: 6.3 g

Mushroom Pizzas

Preparation Time: 10 minutes; Cooking Time: 6 minutes; Servings: 4

Ingredients:
- 4 kalamata olives, sliced
- 2 tablespoons diced sweet red pepper
- 4 large caps of Portobello mushrooms, destemmed
- 3 ounces shredded zucchini
- 2 tablespoons minced basil
- ½ teaspoon minced garlic
- 1 teaspoon ground black pepper
- 2 teaspoons salt
- 1 teaspoon dried basil
- 2 tablespoons balsamic vinegar
- 4 tablespoons pasta sauce
- 1/2 cups hummus
- Olive oil spray

Method:
1. Switch on the air fryer, insert the fryer basket, then shut it with the lid, set the frying temperature 330 degrees F, and let it preheat for 5 minutes.
2. Meanwhile, prepare the mushroom caps, remove the stem and gills, and brush with vinegar.
3. Season mushrooms with half of each salt and black pepper, then spread 1 tablespoon of pasta sauce into each mushroom and sprinkle with garlic.
4. Open the preheated fryer, place mushrooms in it in a single layer, close the lid and cook for 3 minutes.
5. When done, the air fryer will beep, open the lid, take out the mushrooms and top evenly with red pepper, olives, and zucchini, sprinkle with dried basil and remaining black pepper and salt.
6. Return stuffed mushrooms into the baking basket, shut with lid, and continue cooking for 3 minutes until mushrooms are fork-tender.
7. When done, transfer mushrooms to a dish, drizzle with mined basil and hummus and serve.
8. Serve straight away.

Nutrition Value:
- Calories: 70
- Fat: 1.6 g
- Carbs: 11 g
- Protein: 4.3 g
- Fiber: 3.5 g

Green Bean and Mushroom Casserole

Preparation Time: 5 minutes; Cooking Time: 12 minutes; Servings: 6

Ingredients:
- 24 ounces green beans, trimmed
- 1/3 cup fried French onions
- 2 cups sliced button mushrooms
- 1 teaspoon onion powder
- 1 tablespoon garlic powder
- 3/4 teaspoon ground black pepper
- 3/4 teaspoon salt
- 3/4 teaspoon ground sage
- 1 lemon, juiced
- Olive oil spray

Method:
1. Switch on the air fryer, insert the fryer basket, then shut it with the lid, set the frying temperature 400 degrees F, and let it preheat for 5 minutes.
2. Meanwhile, take a large bowl, place all the ingredients in it, except for French onions, and stir until mixed.
3. Open the preheated fryer, place green beans mixture in it, spray with olive oil, close the lid and cook for 12 minutes until golden brown and cooked, shaking halfway.
4. When done, the air fryer will beep and then open the lid and transfer green beans to a dish.
5. Garnish green beans with fried onions and serve straight away.

Nutrition Value:
- Calories: 83
- Fat: 3 g
- Carbs: 12.3 g
- Protein: 2.9 g
- Fiber: 3.4 g

Black Bean Burger

Preparation Time: 20 minutes; Cooking Time: 15 minutes; Servings: 6

Ingredients:
- 1 1/3 cups rolled oats
- 1/2 cup corn kernels
- 12 ounces cooked black beans
- 1/2 teaspoon garlic powder
- 1 1/4 teaspoons red chili powder
- 1 tablespoon soy sauce
- 1/2 teaspoon chipotle chili powder
- 3/4 cup tomato salsa
- Olive oil spray

Method:
1. Switch on the air fryer, insert the fryer basket, then shut it with the lid, set the frying temperature 375 degrees F, and let it preheat for 5 minutes.
2. Meanwhile, take a food processor, add oats in it and pulse for five-time until oats are partially chipped.
3. Then remaining ingredients in it, except for corn, pulse for 1 minute until blended, and tip the mixture in a bowl.
4. Stir in corn, cover the bowl with a plastic wrap, place in the refrigerator for 15 minutes until chilled, and then shape the mixture into six burgers.
5. Open the preheated fryer, place bean burgers in it in a single layer, spray with olive oil, close the lid and cook for 15 minutes until golden brown and cooked, turning and spraying with oil halfway.
6. When done, the air fryer will beep and then open the lid and transfer black bean burgers to a dish.
7. Serve straight away.

Nutrition Value:
- Calories: 158
- Fat: 1.3 g
- Carbs: 30 g
- Protein: 8 g
- Fiber: 9 g

Falafel

Preparation Time: 1 hour and 30 minutes; Cooking Time: 10 minutes; Servings: 8

Ingredients:

- ½ cup white onion, chopped
- 7 cloves garlic
- ½ cup fresh cilantro, chopped
- ½ cup fresh parsley, chopped
- 1 ½ cups dry garbanzo beans, soaked in water overnight
- 2 tablespoons all-purpose flour
- 1 tablespoon ground cumin
- 1 teaspoon ground coriander
- ⅛ teaspoon cayenne pepper
- ⅛ teaspoon ground cardamom
- Salt to taste

Method:

1. Put onion, garlic, cilantro and parsley in a food processor.
2. Pulse until well combined.
3. Add the rest of the ingredients to the food processor.
4. Pulse until consistency is rough and coarse.
5. Put the mixture into a bowl.
6. Cover with foil and refrigerate for 1 hour.
7. Form into patties.
8. Preheat your air fryer to 400 degrees F.
9. Spray air fryer basket with oil.
10. Put the patties in the air fryer basket and cook for 10 minutes.
11. Cook in batches.

Nutritional Value:

- Calories: 150
- Fat: 2.5 g
- Carbs: 25 g
- Fiber: 7 g
- Protein: 8 g

Lentil Balls with Rice

Preparation Time: 10 minutes; Cooking Time: 20 minutes; Servings: 4

Ingredients:

- 30 oz. lentils, rinsed and drained
- 3 tablespoons mushrooms, chopped
- 1 cup walnuts, sliced in half
- 3 tablespoons fresh parsley, chopped
- 1 ½ tablespoons tomato paste
- Salt and pepper to taste
- ½ cup breadcrumbs
- 4 cups cooked rice
- 2 tablespoons lemon juice
- 2 teaspoons lemon zest
- 1 ½ tablespoons fresh parsley, minced
- 2 cups lettuce, chopped
- 1 cup cherry tomatoes, sliced in half
- ¼ cup onion, chopped
- 4 lemon wedges

Method:

1. Put the lentils, mushrooms, walnuts, 3 tablespoons parsley, tomato paste, salt and pepper in a food processor.
2. Pulse until chopped into smaller pieces.
3. Add the breadcrumbs and pulse for a few seconds until well combined.
4. Form balls from the mixture.
5. Cook the lentil balls in the air fryer at 380 degrees F for 10 minutes.
6. In a pan over medium heat, add the cooked rice.
7. Add the lemon juice, lemon zest and remaining parsley.
8. Cook for 5 minutes, stirring frequently.
9. Divide the rice into 4 bowls.
10. Top with the lentil's balls, lettuce, tomato, onion and lemon wedges.

Nutritional Value:

- Calories: 659
- Fat: 20 g
- Carbs: 101 g
- Fiber: 15 g
- Protein: 23 g

Seitan Riblets

Preparation Time: 15 minutes; Cooking Time: 20 minutes; Servings: 4

Ingredients:

- ¼ cup nutritional yeast
- 1 cup vital wheat gluten
- 1 teaspoon onion powder
- 1 teaspoon mushroom powder
- ½ teaspoon garlic powder
- Salt to taste
- ¼ cup barbecue sauce

Method:

1. Add all the ingredients except water and barbecue sauce in the food processor.
2. Pulse until smooth.
3. Knead the dough with your hands and form a round or square shape.
4. Place the seitan pieces in the air fryer.
5. Cook at 370 degrees F for 8 minutes.
6. Flip and then cook for another 5 minutes.
7. Drizzle with barbecue sauce before serving.

Nutritional Value:

- Calories: 93
- Fat: 0.7g
- Carbs: 12.7g
- Fiber: 2.7g
- Protein: 10.5g

Lasagna

Preparation Time: 9 minutes; Cooking Time: 21 minutes; Servings: 1

Ingredients:

- 2 lasagna noodles, broken in half
- Salt to taste
- ½ cup pasta sauce
- ¼ cup vegan cheese
- 1 cup fresh basil, chopped
- ¼ cup baby spinach, chopped
- 1 handful baby spinach leaves chopped, about 1/4 cup chopped
- 3 tablespoons zucchini, shredded

Method:

1. Boil the lasagna noodles according to directions in the package.
2. Drain the noodles.
3. In a loaf pan, spread a tablespoon of the pasta sauce.
4. Top it with the lasagna noodle.
5. Put layers of cheese, basil, spinach and zucchini on top.
6. Add another lasagna noodle and repeat the layers until you've used up all the noodles.
7. Cover the pan with foil.
8. Put inside the air fryer.
9. Cook at 400 degrees F for 10 minutes.
10. Remove the foil.
11. Cook for another 5 minutes.

Nutritional Value:

- Calories: 344
- Fat: 9 g
- Carbs: 52 g
- Fiber: 3 g
- Protein: 14 g

Italian Tofu

Preparation Time: 10 minutes; Cooking Time: 10 minutes; Servings: 2

Ingredients:

- 8 oz. tofu, sliced lengthwise
- 1 tablespoon tamari
- 1 tablespoon broth
- ½ teaspoon dried oregano
- ½ teaspoon dried basil
- ½ teaspoon granulated garlic
- ¼ teaspoon granulated onion
- Pepper to taste

Method:

1. Drain the tofu slices with paper towel.
2. Mix the rest of the ingredients in a bowl.
3. Coat the tofu with the mixture and marinate for 10 minutes.
4. Preheat your air fryer to 400 degrees F.
5. Cook the tofu in the air fryer for 6 minutes.
6. Flip and then cook for another 4 minutes.
7. Serve with pasta or vegetables.

Nutritional Value:

- Calories: 87
- Fat: 4.4 g
- Carbs: 3.4 g
- Fiber: 1.3 g
- Protein: 10 g

Eggplant Parmesan

Preparation Time: 10 minutes; Cooking Time: 20 minutes; Servings: 6

Ingredients:
- 2 tablespoons vegan Parmesan cheese, grated
- ½ cup breadcrumbs
- Garlic powder to taste
- Onion powder to taste
- Salt and pepper to taste
- 1 eggplant, sliced
- ½ cup flour
- ½ cup almond milk
- Cooking spray
- 1 cup marinara sauce
- ½ cup vegan mozzarella, shredded
- Parsley, chopped

Method:
1. In a bowl, mix the Parmesan cheese, breadcrumbs, garlic powder, onion powder, salt and pepper.
2. Dip each eggplant slice in flour, then dip into the almond milk and then cover with Parmesan and breadcrumb mixture.
3. Spray air fryer basket with oil.
4. Cook the eggplant in the air fryer at 390 degrees F for 15 minutes, flipping halfway through.
5. Top with marinara sauce, mozzarella and parsley before serving.

Nutritional Value:
- Calories: 176
- Fat: 6.7g
- Carbs: 25.9g
- Fiber: 4.9g
- Protein: 4.3g

Buffalo Cauliflower

Preparation Time: 10 minutes; Cooking Time: 12 minutes; Servings: 4

Ingredients:

- 1 cauliflower, sliced into florets
- 2 tablespoons hot sauce
- 1 ½ teaspoons maple syrup
- 2 teaspoons avocado oil
- 2 tablespoons nutritional yeast
- Salt to taste
- 1 tablespoon arrowroot starch

Method:

1. Preheat your fryer to 360 degrees F.
2. In a bowl, put all the ingredients except the cauliflower.
3. Mix well.
4. Toss cauliflower into the mixture to coat evenly.
5. Cook in the air fryer for 14 minutes, shaking halfway during the cooking.

Nutritional Value:

- Calories: 52
- Fat: 0.7g
- Carbs: 9.5g
- Fiber: 3.1g
- Protein: 3.7g

Lemon Tofu

Preparation Time: 15 minutes; Cooking Time: 25 minutes; Servings: 4

Ingredients:

- 1 lb. tofu, sliced into cubes
- 1 tablespoon tamari
- 1 tablespoon arrowroot powder
- ¼ cup lemon juice
- 1 teaspoon lemon zest
- 2 tablespoon sugar
- ½ cup water
- aspoons cornstarch

Method:

1. Coat the tofu cubes in tamari.
2. Dredge with arrowroot powder.
3. Let sit for 15 minutes.
4. Add the rest of the ingredients in a bowl, mix and set aside.
5. Cook the tofu in the air fryer at 390 degrees F for 10 minutes, shaking halfway through.
6. Put the tofu in a skillet over medium high heat.
7. Stir in the sauce.
8. Simmer until the sauce has thickened.
9. Serve with rice or vegetables.

Nutritional Value:

- Calories: 112
- Fat: 3 g
- Carbs: 13 g
- Fiber: 6 g
- Protein: 8 g

Tofu Buddha Bowl

Preparation Time: 15 minutes; Cooking Time: 35 minutes; Servings: 6

Ingredients:

- ¼ cup soy sauce
- 2 tablespoons sesame oil
- 2 tablespoons lime juice
- 1 tablespoon hot sauce
- 3 tablespoons molasses
- 14 oz. tofu, cubed
- Cooking spray
- 1 lb. fresh broccoli florets
- 1 red bell pepper, sliced thinly
- 3 carrots, sliced thinly
- 8 oz. fresh spinach
- 1 teaspoon garlic, minced
- 1 tablespoon olive oil
- 2 cups cooked quinoa

Method:

1. In a bowl, mix the soy sauce, oil, lime juice, hot sauce and molasses.
2. Marinate tofu for 10 minutes.
3. Spray air fryer basket with oil.
4. Cook tofu in the air fryer at 370 degrees F for 15 minutes. Shake every 5 minutes.
5. Add broccoli, bell pepper and carrots in the marinade.
6. Marinate for 10 minutes.
7. In a pan over medium heat, sauté the garlic in olive oil and add the spinach.
8. Cook until the spinach has wilted but do not overcook.
9. Cook the marinated vegetables in the air fryer for 10 minutes, shaking once or twice halfway through.
10. In a serving bowl, put the quinoa and then arrange the tofu, vegetables and spinach.

Nutritional Value:

- Calories: 236
- Fat: 8 g
- Carbs: 31 g
- Fiber: 6 g
- Protein: 12 g

Chickpea Tacos

Preparation Time: 10 minutes; Cooking Time: 20 minutes; Servings: 4

Ingredients:

- 19 oz. canned chickpeas, rinsed and drained
- 4 cups cauliflower florets, chopped
- 2 tablespoons olive oil
- 2 tablespoons taco seasoning
- 4 tortillas
- 4 cups cabbage, shredded
- 2 avocados, sliced
- Soy yogurt

Method:

1. Preheat your air fryer to 390 degrees F.
2. Toss the chickpeas and cauliflower in olive oil.
3. Sprinkle with taco seasoning.
4. Put in the air fryer basket.
5. Cook for 20 minutes, shaking occasionally.
6. Stuff filling into the tortillas and top with cabbage, avocado and yogurt.

Nutritional Value:

- Calories: 464
- Fat: 18.6g
- Carbs: 61.3g
- Fiber: 18.2g
- Protein: 17.3g

Fish Taco Wraps

Preparation Time: 5 minutes; Cooking Time: 12 minutes; Servings: 4

Ingredients:
- 2 cobs of grilled corns
- 1 small white onion, peeled, diced
- 4 pieces of Fishless Filet
- 1 small red bell pepper, cored, deseeded, diced
- 4 large tortillas, burrito-size
- ½ cup Mango Salsa
- Mixed green as needed
- Tortilla chips as needed
- 4 tablespoons shredded vegan parmesan cheese
- Olive oil spray

Method:
1. Switch on the air fryer, insert the fryer basket, then shut it with the lid, set the frying temperature 400 degrees F, and let it preheat for 5 minutes.
2. Then open the preheated fryer, place fillets in it in a single layer, spray with olive oil, close the lid and cook for 6 minutes until golden brown and cooked, turning and spraying with oil halfway.
3. Meanwhile, take a skillet pan, place it over medium heat, grease it with oil and when hot, add onion and bell pepper and cook for 5 minutes until softened.
4. Then stir in corn until mixed, continue cooking for 2 minutes until hot, and set aside until required.
5. When done, the air fryer will beep, then open the lid and transfer fillets to a dish.
6. Assemble tacos and for this, evenly spoon one-fourth of the cooked onion-pepper mixture into a tortilla, top with a fish fillet, 2 tablespoons of mango salsa, tortilla chips, mixed greens and grated cheese in the end.
7. Place prepared tacos into the fryer basket, shut with lid, and cook at 350 degrees F for 6 minutes until cooked.
8. Serve straight away.

Nutrition Value:
- Calories: 407
- Fat: 6.4 g
- Carbs: 74.4 g
- Protein: 19.7 g
- Fiber: 24.7 g

Tempeh Kabobs

Preparation Time: 2 hours and 5 minutes; Cooking Time: 20 minutes; Servings: 4

Ingredients:
- 8 ounces tempeh, steamed
- 1 cup sliced button mushrooms
- 1 medium red onion, peeled, quartered
- 1 cup cherry tomato halves
- 1 small green bell pepper, cored, sliced
- Olive oil spray
- Soaked wooden skewers

For the Marinade:
- 1 ½ teaspoons minced garlic
- 1/2 teaspoon ground black pepper
- 2 teaspoons ground cumin
- 1 teaspoon maple syrup
- 1 teaspoon ground turmeric
- 2 lemons, juiced
- 1/4 cup soy sauce
- 2 teaspoons olive oil
- 3/4 cup vegetable broth

Method:
1. Prepare the marinade, and for this, take a bowl, place all of its ingredients in it and whisk until combined.
2. Cut steamed tempeh into twelve cubes, place them in a large container, add vegetables, then pour in half of the prepared marinade, toss until coated, cover the container with a lid and marinate in the refrigerator for 2 hours.
3. Then switch on the air fryer, insert the fryer basket, then shut it with the lid, set the frying temperature 390 degrees F, and let it preheat for 5 minutes.
4. Meanwhile, remove tempeh cubes and vegetables from the marinade, thread tempeh alternating with vegetables onto skewers, reserving the marinade.
5. Open the preheated fryer, place skewers in it in a single layer, spray with olive oil, close the lid, cook for 5 minutes, then brush with the marinade, turn them and continue cooking for another 5 minutes until thoroughly cooked.
6. When done, the air fryer will beep, open the lid, transfer kabobs to a dish, and cover with foil to keep them warm.
7. Cook remaining kabobs in the same manner and serve.

Nutrition Value:
- Calories: 173.2
- Fat: 2.8 g
- Carbs: 36.5 g
- Protein: 5 g

- Fiber: 7.7 g

Barbecue Soy Curls

Preparation Time: 13 minutes; Cooking Time: 8 minutes; Servings: 2

Ingredients:

- 1 cup soy curls
- 1 cup warm water
- 1 teaspoon vegan bouillon
- ¼ cup barbecue sauce

Method:

1. Soak the soy curls in water and bouillon for 10 minutes.
2. Drain and squeeze out excess water.
3. Shred soy curls.
4. Cook in the air fryer at 400 degrees F for 3 minutes.
5. Toss in barbecue sauce and then put back in the air fryer.
6. Cook for another 5 minutes, shaking the basket twice.

Nutritional Value:

- Calories: 136
- Fat: 3 g
- Carbs: 18 g
- Fiber: 2 g
- Protein: 7 g

Cauliflower and Chickpea Tacos

Preparation Time: 10 minutes; Cooking Time: 20 minutes; Servings: 4

Ingredients:
- 19 ounces cooked chickpeas
- 4 cups cauliflower florets, chopped
- 2 tablespoons taco seasoning
- 2 tablespoons olive oil

For Serving:
- 2 medium avocados, peeled, pitted, sliced
- Coconut yogurt as needed for drizzle
- 4 cups shredded cabbage
- 8 small tortillas

Method:
1. Switch on the air fryer, insert the fryer basket, then shut it with the lid, set the frying temperature 390 degrees F, and let it preheat for 5 minutes.
2. Meanwhile, take a large bowl, add cauliflower florets and chickpeas, sprinkle with taco seasoning, drizzle with oil and toss until combined.
3. Open the preheated fryer, place cauliflower-chickpeas in it in a single layer, close the lid and cook for 20 minutes until golden brown and cooked, shaking oil halfway.
4. When done, the air fryer will beep, then open the lid and transfer cauliflower-chickpeas mixture to a dish.
5. Distribute transfer cauliflower-chickpeas mixture evenly between tortillas, top with cabbage and avocado, drizzle with yogurt, and serve.

Nutrition Value:
- Calories: 190
- Fat: 16 g
- Carbs: 11 g
- Protein: 3 g
- Fiber: 3 g

"Crab" Cake

Preparation Time: 20 minutes; Cooking Time: 15 minutes; Servings: 8

Ingredients:

- 5 potatoes, diced
- 2 stalks green onion, chopped
- 1 teaspoon lemon juice
- ½ teaspoon lemon zest
- 1 teaspoon ginger, grated
- 1 tablespoon soy sauce
- 4 tablespoons red curry paste
- Salt and pepper to taste
- Cooking spray

Method:

1. Put all the ingredients in a food processor.
2. Pulse until tender and well combined.
3. Drain and then form into patties.
4. Spray air fryer basket with oil.
5. Cook at 400 degrees F for 20 to 25 minutes until fully cooked. Flip halfway through the cooking.

Nutritional Value:

- Calories: 97
- Fat: 1 g
- Carbs: 25 g
- Fiber: 5 g
- Protein: 4 g

Sweet & Spicy Cauliflower

Preparation Time: 10 minutes; Cooking Time: 30 minutes; Servings: 4

Ingredients:

- 4 cups cauliflower florets
- 1 onion, chopped
- 5 cloves garlic, chopped
- 1 ½ tablespoons tamari
- 1 tablespoon rice vinegar
- ½ teaspoon coconut sugar
- 1 tablespoon hot sauce
- 2 scallions, chopped

Method:

1. Put the cauliflower in the air fryer basket.
2. Cook at 350 degrees F for 10 minutes, shaking halfway through.
3. Add the onion and cook for another 10 minutes.
4. Add the garlic and stir.
5. Cook for 5 more minutes.
6. In a bowl, mix all the ingredients except the scallions.
7. Add to the air fryer. Mix well.
8. Cook for 5 minutes.
9. Sprinkle scallions on top before serving.

Nutritional Value:

- Calories: 93
- Fat: 3 g
- Carbs: 12 g
- Fiber: 3 g
- Protein: 4 g

Mushroom & Green Bean Casserole

Preparation Time: 10 minutes; Cooking Time: 10 minutes; Servings: 6

Ingredients:

- 24 oz. green beans, trimmed
- 2 cups button mushrooms, sliced
- 1 tablespoon lemon juice
- 1 tablespoon garlic powder
- ¾ teaspoon ground sage
- 1 teaspoon onion powder
- Salt and pepper to taste
- Cooking spray

Method:

1. Combine all the ingredients in a bowl.
2. Transfer to the air fryer basket and coat with oil.
3. Cook at 400 degrees F for 12 minutes.
4. Shake every 3 minutes.

Nutritional Value:

- Calories: 47
- Fat: 0.3g
- Carbs: 10.3g
- Fiber: 4.3g
- Protein: 3.1g

Cauliflower Steak

Preparation Time: 5 minutes; Cooking Time: 15 minutes; Servings: 6

Ingredients:

- 2 heads cauliflower, green leaves removed, sliced into thick "steaks"
- 2 tablespoons coconut oil
- Salt and pepper to taste
- ¼ teaspoon ground ginger
- 1 teaspoon ground turmeric
- Tahini
- Sesame seeds
- Steamed green beans

Method:

1. Coat the cauliflower steaks with oil and season with salt, pepper, ginger and turmeric.
2. Place in the air fryer and cook at 390 degrees F for 15 minutes. Flip halfway through.
3. Drizzle with tahini and sesame seeds.
4. Serve with green beans.

Nutritional Value:

- Calories: 66
- Fat: 4.7g
- Carbs: 5.6g
- Fiber: 2.6g
- Protein: 2g

Chapter 7: Vegetable and Sides Recipes

Maple Roasted Brussels sprouts

Preparation Time: 5 minutes; Cooking Time: 10 minutes; Servings: 2

Ingredients:
- 2 cups Brussels sprouts, ¼-inch thick sliced
- 1/4 teaspoon sea salt
- 1 tablespoon balsamic vinegar
- 1 tablespoon maple syrup

Method:
1. Switch on the air fryer, insert the fryer basket, then shut it with the lid, set the frying temperature 400 degrees F, and let it preheat for 5 minutes.
2. Meanwhile, take a large bowl, add Brussel sprouts in it, season with salt, drizzle with vinegar and maple syrup and toss until well coated.
3. Open the preheated fryer, place Brussel sprouts in it, close the lid and cook for 10 minutes until golden brown and cooked, shaking halfway.
4. When done, the air fryer will beep, then open the lid and transfer Brussel sprouts to a dish.
5. Serve straight away.

Nutrition Value:
- Calories: 85.3
- Fat: 3.3 g
- Carbs: 13.1 g
- Protein: 2.8 g
- Fiber: 2.8 g

Roasted Butternut Squash with Mushrooms and Cranberries

Preparation Time: 5 minutes; Cooking Time: 30 minutes; Servings: 6

Ingredients:
- 4 cups diced butternut squash
- 1 cup sliced green onions
- 8 ounces button mushrooms, destemmed, quartered
- ¼ cup dried cranberries

For the Sauce:
- 1 tablespoon maple syrup
- 4 cloves of garlic, peeled
- 1 tablespoon soy sauce
- 1 tablespoon balsamic vinegar
- 1 tablespoon olive oil

Method:
1. Switch on the air fryer, insert the fryer basket, then shut it with the lid, set the frying temperature 400 degrees F, and let it preheat for 5 minutes.
2. Meanwhile, prepare the sauce and for this, place all of its ingredients in a food processor and puree for 1 minute until blended.
3. Take a large bowl, place all the vegetables and berries, add sauce and toss until coated.
4. Open the preheated fryer, place vegetables in it, close the lid and cook for 30 minutes until golden brown and cooked, shaking every 10 minutes.
5. When done, the air fryer will beep, then open the lid, transfer vegetables and berries to a dish and garnish with some more green onions.
6. Serve straight away.

Nutrition Value:
- Calories: 128
- Fat: 2.6 g
- Carbs: 28 g
- Protein: 2.2 g
- Fiber: 8.6 g

Corn and Zucchini Fritters

Preparation Time: 5 minutes; Cooking Time: 16 minutes; Servings: 4

Ingredients:
- 2 medium zucchini, grated, moisture squeezed out
- 1 medium potato, peeled, grated, cooked
- 2 tablespoons chickpea flour
- 1 teaspoon minced garlic
- ½ teaspoon ground black pepper
- 1 teaspoon salt
- 1 cup corn kernels
- 2 teaspoons olive oil

Method:
1. Switch on the air fryer, insert the fryer basket, then shut it with the lid, set the frying temperature 360 degrees F, and let it preheat for 5 minutes.
2. Meanwhile, take a large bowl, add all the ingredients in it, except for oil, stir until combined, then shape the mixture into small twelve patties, each about 2 tablespoons of the batter and brush them with oil on both sides.
3. Open the preheated fryer, place patties in it in a single layer, and cook for 8 minutes until golden brown and cooked, turning halfway.
4. When done, the air fryer will beep, open the lid, transfer fritters to a dish, and cover with foil to keep them warm.
5. Cook remaining patties in the same manner and serve straight away.

Nutrition Value:
- Calories: 114.1
- Fat: 6.1 g
- Carbs: 12.8 g
- Protein: 2.6 g
- Fiber: 0.9 g

Roasted Corn

Preparation Time: 5 minutes; Cooking Time: 10 minutes; Servings: 4

Ingredients:
- 4 ears of corn, husk removed
- ½ teaspoon ground black pepper
- 1 teaspoon salt
- 3 teaspoons olive oil

Method:
1. Switch on the air fryer, insert the fryer basket, then shut it with the lid, set the frying temperature 400 degrees F, and let it preheat for 5 minutes.
2. Meanwhile, remove husk and silk from corn, rinse them well, and pat dry.
3. Then cut the corns to fit into the fryer basket, drizzle with oil and season with black pepper and salt.
4. Open the preheated fryer, place corns in it, close the lid and cook for 10 minutes until golden brown and cooked, turning halfway.
5. When done, the air fryer will beep and then open the lid and transfer corn to a dish.
6. Serve straight away.

Nutrition Value:
- Calories: 175
- Fat: 7.7 g
- Carbs: 27 g
- Protein: 4.8 g
- Fiber: 3 g

Roasted Green Beans

Preparation Time: 5 minutes; Cooking Time: 10 minutes; Servings: 2

Ingredients:
- 8 ounces green beans, trimmed
- 1 teaspoon sesame oil
- 1 tablespoon soy sauce

Method:
1. Switch on the air fryer, insert the fryer basket, then shut it with the lid, set the frying temperature 400 degrees F, and let it preheat for 5 minutes.
2. Meanwhile, snap the green beans into half, place them in a large bowl, add oil and soy sauce and toss until well coated.
3. Open the preheated fryer, place green beans in it, spray with olive oil, close the lid and cook for 10 minutes until golden brown and cooked, shaking halfway.
4. When done, the air fryer will beep and then open the lid and transfer green beans to a dish.
5. Serve straight away.

Nutrition Value:
- Calories: 33.2
- Fat: 2.5 g
- Carbs: 2.7 g
- Protein: 0.7 g
- Fiber: 1.3 g

Shishito Peppers

Preparation Time: 5 minutes; Cooking Time: 6 minutes; Servings: 4

Ingredients:
- 20 Shishito peppers
- 1 teaspoon salt
- Olive oil spray

Method:
1. Switch on the air fryer, insert the fryer basket, then shut it with the lid, set the frying temperature 390 degrees F, and let it preheat for 5 minutes.
2. Open the preheated fryer, place peppers in it, spray well with olive oil, close the lid and cook for 6 minutes until cooked and lightly charred, shaking halfway.
3. When done, the air fryer will beep, open the lid, transfer peppers to a dish, and season with salt.
4. Serve straight away.

Nutrition Value:
- Calories: 21
- Fat: 1 g
- Carbs: 5 g
- Protein: 1 g
- Fiber: 2 g

Cheesy Potatoes

Preparation Time: 5 minutes; Cooking Time: 18 minutes; Servings: 4

Ingredients:

For the Potatoes:
- 1 pound fingerling potatoes, washed, halved
- 1 teaspoon ground black pepper
- 1/2 teaspoon garlic powder
- 1 teaspoon salt
- 1 teaspoon olive oil

For the Cheese Sauce:
- 2 tablespoons nutritional yeast
- 1/2 teaspoon paprika
- 1/2 teaspoon ground turmeric
- 1/2 cup cashews
- 1 teaspoon lemon juice
- 1/4 cup water

Method:
1. Switch on the air fryer, insert the fryer basket, then shut it with the lid, set the frying temperature 400 degrees F, and let it preheat for 5 minutes.
2. Meanwhile, prepare the potatoes and for this, cut each potato into half, place them in a large bowl, all remaining ingredients in it, and toss until coated.
3. Open the preheated fryer, place potatoes in it, close the lid and cook for 16 minutes until golden brown and cooked, shaking halfway.
4. Meanwhile, prepare the cheese sauce and, for this, place all of its ingredients in a food processor, except for water, and blend on low until combined.
5. Then slowly blend in water until sauce reaches to desired consistency and set it aside until required.
6. When done, the air fryer will beep, open the lid, transfer potato wedges to a fryer baking pan, and drizzle with cheese sauce.
7. Insert baking pan into the air fryer, shut with lid, and cook at 400 degrees F for 2 minutes.
8. Serve straight away.

Nutrition Value:
- Calories: 238
- Fat: 12.5 g
- Carbs: 25 g
- Protein: 8.5 g
- Fiber: 3.8 g

Roasted Garlic

Preparation Time: 10 minutes; Cooking Time: 25 minutes; Servings: 4

Ingredients:
- 1 medium head of garlic
- Olive oil spray

Method:
1. Switch on the air fryer, insert the fryer basket, then shut it with the lid, set the frying temperature 400 degrees F, and let it preheat for 5 minutes.
2. Meanwhile, remove excess peel from the garlic head, and then expose the top of garlic by removing ¼-inch off the top.
3. Spray the garlic head with oil generously and then wrap with a foil.
4. Open the preheated fryer, place wrapped garlic head in it, close the lid and cook for 25 minutes until done.
5. When done, the air fryer will beep, then open the lid, transfer garlic to a dish and let it cool for 5 minutes.
6. Then squeeze the garlic out of its skin and serve with warmed garlic or as desired.

Nutrition Value:
- Calories: 160
- Fat: 2.5 g
- Carbs: 27 g
- Protein: 6 g
- Fiber: 3 g

Kale Chips

Preparation Time: 5 minutes; Cooking Time: 10 minutes; Servings: 2

Ingredients:

- Cooking spray
- 6 cups kale leaves, torn
- 1 tablespoon olive oil
- Salt to taste
- 1 ½ teaspoons low- soy sauce
- ¼ teaspoon ground cumin
- ½ teaspoon white sesame seeds

Method:

1. Spray air fryer basket with oil.
2. Toss kale in oil, salt and soy sauce.
3. Cook at 375 degrees F for 10 minutes or until crispy. Shake every 3 minutes.
4. Sprinkle with cumin and sesame seeds before serving.

Nutritional Value:

- Calories: 140
- Fat: 9 g
- Carbs: 13 g
- Fiber: 4 g
- Protein: 4 g

Baby Bok Choy

Preparation Time: 5 minutes; Cooking Time: 6 minutes; Servings: 4

Ingredients:
- 4 bunches of babies bok choy
- 1 teaspoon garlic powder
- Olive oil spray

Method:
1. Switch on the air fryer, insert the fryer basket, then shut it with the lid, set the frying temperature 350 degrees F, and let it preheat for 5 minutes.
2. Meanwhile, prepare the bok choy and for this, slice off the bottom, separate the leaves, rinse and drain well.
3. Open the preheated fryer, place bok choy in it, spray generously with olive oil, sprinkle with garlic powder, shake well, close the lid and cook for 6 minutes until golden brown and cooked, shaking halfway.
4. When done, the air fryer will beep, then open the lid and transfer bok choy to a dish.
5. Serve straight away.

Nutrition Value:
- Calories: 58
- Fat: 2 g
- Carbs: 5 g
- Protein: 1 g
- Fiber: 1 g

Plantain Chips

Preparation Time: 5 minutes; Cooking Time: 20 minutes; Servings: 2

Ingredients:
- 3 green plantains, peeled, sliced
- 1 lime, zested
- ½ teaspoon garlic powder
- 1 teaspoon of sea salt
- 1/8 teaspoon red chili powder
- 2 teaspoons olive oil
- 1 cup guacamole, for serving

Method:
1. Switch on the air fryer, insert the fryer basket, then shut it with the lid, set the frying temperature 374 degrees F, and let it preheat for 5 minutes.
2. Meanwhile, take a large bowl, add plantain slices in it along with remaining ingredients, except for guacamole and toss until coated.
3. Open the preheated fryer, place plantain in it, close the lid and cook for 20 minutes until golden brown and cooked, shaking every 5 minutes.
4. When done, the air fryer will beep and then open the lid and transfer plantain chips to a dish.
5. Serve plantain chips with guacamole.

Nutrition Value:
- Calories: 220
- Fat: 12 g
- Carbs: 25 g
- Protein: 1 g
- Fiber: 2 g

Popcorn Tofu

Preparation Time: 5 minutes; Cooking Time: 24 minutes; Servings: 4

Ingredients:
- 14 ounces tofu, extra-firm, pressed, drained
- 1 ½ cup panko bread crumbs

For the Batter:
- 1 teaspoon onion powder
- 1/2 cup cornmeal
- 1/2 cup chickpea flour
- 1 teaspoon garlic powder
- 1/2 teaspoon ground black pepper
- 1/2 teaspoon salt
- 1 tablespoon Vegetarian Bouillon
- 2 tablespoons nutritional yeast
- 1 tablespoon Dijon mustard
- 3/4 cup almond milk, unsweetened

Method:
1. Switch on the air fryer, insert the fryer basket, then shut it with the lid, set the frying temperature 350 degrees F, and let it preheat for 5 minutes.
2. Meanwhile, prepare the batter and for this, place all of its ingredients in a large bowl and then whisk until combined until smooth batter comes together.
3. Take a shallow dish and then place bread crumbs in it.
4. Cut tofu into bite-size pieces, dip into prepared batter and then dredge with bread crumbs until coated on both sides.
5. Open the preheated fryer, place tofu in it in a single layer, spray with olive oil, close the lid and cook for 12 minutes until golden brown and cooked, shaking halfway.
6. When done, the air fryer will beep, open the lid, transfer popcorns to a dish, and cover with foil to keep them warm.
7. Cook remaining tofu popcorns in the same manner and then serve.

Nutrition Value:
- Calories: 261
- Fat: 5.5 g
- Carbs: 37.5 g
- Protein: 16 g
- Fiber: 4.8 g

Crispy Vegetables

Preparation Time: 15 minutes; Cooking Time: 8 minutes; Servings: 4

Ingredients:

- 1 cup rice flour
- 1 tablespoon nutritional yeast flakes
- 2 tablespoons vegan egg powder
- 2/3 cup cold water
- 1 cup breadcrumbs
- Salt and pepper to taste
- 1 cup squash, sliced into strips
- 1 cup zucchini, sliced into strips
- ½ cup green beans
- ½ cup cauliflower, sliced into florets
- Cooking spray

Method:

1. Set up three bowls.
2. One is for the rice flour, another for the egg powder, nutritional yeast and water, another for the breadcrumbs.
3. Dip each of the vegetable slices in the first, second and third bowls.
4. Spray the air fryer basket with oil.
5. Cook at 380 degrees F for 8 minutes or until crispy.

Nutritional Value:

- Calories: 272
- Fat: 2.2g
- Carbs: 54.8g
- Fiber: 3.9g
- Protein: 7.9g

Baked Potatoes with Broccoli & Cheese

Preparation Time: 10 minutes; Cooking Time: 30 minutes; Servings: 8

Ingredients:

- 4 potatoes
- 1 cup almond milk, divided
- 2 tablespoons all-purpose flour
- ½ cup vegan cheese, divided
- 1 cup broccoli, florets, chopped
- Salt to taste
- Chopped onion chives

Method:

1. Poke all sides of potatoes with a fork.
2. Microwave on high level for 5 minutes.
3. Flip and microwave for another 5 minutes.
4. In a saucepan over medium heat, heat ¾ cup of milk for 2 minutes, stirring frequently.
5. Add the remaining milk in a bowl and stir in the flour.
6. Add this mixture to the pan and bring to a boil.
7. Reduce heat
8. Reserve 2 tablespoons vegan cheese.
9. Add the rest of the cheese to the pan and stir until smooth.
10. Add the broccoli, salt and cayenne.
11. Cook for 1 minute and remove from heat.
12. Slice the potatoes and arrange on a single layer inside the air fryer.
13. Top with the broccoli mixture.
14. Add another layer of potatoes and broccoli mixture.
15. Sprinkle reserved cheese on top.
16. Cook at 350 degrees F for 5 minutes.
17. Garnish with chopped chives.

Nutritional Value:

- Calories: 137
- Fat: 3 g
- Carbs: 148 g
- Fiber: 2 g
- Protein: 5 g

Roasted Spicy Carrots

Preparation Time: 5 minutes; Cooking Time: 15 minutes; Servings: 4

Ingredients:

- ½ lb. carrots, sliced
- ½ tablespoon olive oil
- Salt to taste
- 1/8 teaspoon garlic powder
- ¼ teaspoon chili powder
- 1 teaspoon ground cumin
- Sesame seeds
- Fresh cilantro

Method:

1. Preheat your air fryer at 390 degrees F for 5 minutes.
2. Cook the carrots at 390 degrees F for 10 minutes.
3. Transfer to a bowl.
4. Mix the oil, salt, garlic powder, chili powder and ground cumin.
5. Coat the carrots with the oil mixture.
6. Put the carrots back to the air fryer and cook for another 5 minutes.
7. Garnish with sesame seeds and cilantro.

Nutritional Value:

- Calories: 82
- Fat: 3.8g
- Carbs: 11.9g
- Fiber: 3g
- Protein: 1.2g

Avocado Fries

Preparation Time: 10 minutes; Cooking Time: 10 minutes; Servings: 4

Ingredients:

- Salt to taste
- ½ cup panko breadcrumbs
- 1 cup aquafaba liquid
- 1 avocado, sliced into strips

Method:

1. Mix the salt and breadcrumbs in a bowl.
2. In another bowl, pour the aquafaba liquid.
3. Dip each avocado strip into the liquid and then dredge with breadcrumbs.
4. Air fry at 390 degrees F for 10 minutes, shaking halfway through.

Nutritional Value:

- Calories: 111
- Fat: 9.9g
- Carbs: 6.2g
- Fiber: 3.6g
- Protein: 1.2g

Baked Tofu Strips

Preparation Time: 30 minutes; Cooking Time: 40 minutes; Servings: 4

Ingredients:

- 2 tablespoons olive oil
- ½ teaspoon oregano
- ½ teaspoon basil
- ¼ teaspoon cayenne pepper
- ¼ teaspoon paprika
- ¼ teaspoon garlic powder
- ¼ teaspoon onion powder
- Salt and pepper to taste
- 15 oz. tofu, drained

Method:

1. Combine all the ingredients except the tofu.
2. Mix well.
3. Slice tofu into strips and dry with paper towel.
4. Marinate in the mixture for 10 minutes.
5. Cook in the air fryer at 375 degrees F for 15 minutes, shaking halfway through.

Nutritional Value:

- Calories: 132
- Fat: 10 g
- Carbs: 3 g
- Fiber: 0 g
- Protein: 7 g

Baked Artichoke Fries

Preparation Time: 10 minutes; Cooking Time: 10 minutes; Servings: 4

Ingredients:

- 14 oz. canned artichoke hearts, drained, rinsed and sliced into wedges
- 1 cup all-purpose flour
- ½ cup almond milk
- ½ teaspoon garlic powder
- Salt and pepper to taste
- 1 ½ cup breadcrumbs
- ½ teaspoon paprika

Method:

1. Dry the artichoke hearts by pressing a paper towel on top.
2. In a bowl, mix the flour, milk, garlic powder, salt and pepper.
3. In a shallow dish, add the paprika and breadcrumbs.
4. Dip each artichoke wedge in the first bowl and then coat with the breadcrumb mixture.
5. Cook at 450 degrees for 10 minutes.
6. Serve fries with your choice of dipping sauce.

Nutritional Value:

- Calories: 391
- Fat: 9.8g
- Carbs: 65.5g
- Fiber: 8.8g
- Protein: 12.7g

Spicy Sweet Potato Fries

Preparation Time: 5 minutes; Cooking Time: 25 minutes; Servings: 6

Ingredients:
- 2 large sweet potatoes, peeled
- 2 teaspoons olive oil

For the Seasoning Mix:
- 2 teaspoons salt
- 1 teaspoon ground fennel
- 2 teaspoons ground coriander
- 1 teaspoon Aleppo pepper
- 1 teaspoon dried oregano

Method:
1. Switch on the air fryer, insert the fryer basket, then shut it with the lid, set the frying temperature 350 degrees F, and let it preheat for 5 minutes.
2. Meanwhile, prepare the fries and for this, cut sweet potatoes into ½-inch fries, place them in a large bowl, and then drizzle with oil.
3. Prepare the seasoning mix, and for this, place all of its ingredients in a blender and pulse until ground.
4. Sprinkle the ground seasoning over sweet potatoes and then toss until well coated.
5. Open the preheated fryer, place sweet potatoes fries in it, close the lid and cook for 25 minutes until golden brown and cooked, shaking halfway.
6. When done, the air fryer will beep and then open the lid and transfer chips to a dish.
7. Serve straight away.

Nutrition Value:
- Calories: 34.4
- Fat: 0.1 g
- Carbs: 7.9 g
- Protein: 0.5 g
- Fiber: 1 g

French Fries

Preparation Time: 40 minutes; Cooking Time: 30 minutes; Servings: 3

Ingredients:

- 2 potatoes, sliced into thick strips
- 1 bowl water
- 2 tablespoons olive oil
- Salt and pepper to taste
- ¼ teaspoon paprika
- 1 tablespoon cornstarch
- Cooking spray
- Green onion, chopped

Method:
1. Soak potato strips in water for 30 minutes.
2. Drain and pat try.
3. Toss in olive oil.
4. Season with salt, pepper and paprika.
5. Cover with cornstarch.
6. Spray air fryer basket with oil.
7. Cook at 360 degrees F for 30 minutes shaking every 5 minutes.
8. Garnish with green onion.

Nutritional Value:
- Calories: 185
- Fat: 9 g
- 297 mg
- Carbs: 23 g
- Fiber: 2 g
- Protein: 2 g

Rosemary Potatoes

Preparation Time: 15 minutes; Cooking Time: 15 minutes; Servings: 4

Ingredients:

- 4 potatoes, cubed
- 1 tablespoon oil
- 1 tablespoon garlic, minced
- 2 teaspoons dried rosemary, minced
- Salt and pepper to taste
- 1 tablespoon lime juice
- ¼ cup parsley, chopped

Method:

1. Toss potato cubes in oil and season with garlic, rosemary, salt and pepper.
2. Put in the air fryer.
3. Cook at 400 degrees F for 15 minutes.
4. Stir in lime juice and top with parsley before serving.

Nutritional Value:

- Calories: 244
- Fat: 10.5g
- Carbs: 35g
- Fiber: 5.6g
- Protein: 3.9g

Crispy Zucchini Wedges

Preparation Time: 10 minutes; Cooking Time: 12 minutes; Servings: 6

Ingredients:
- Cooking spray
- ½ cup all-purpose flour
- 2 vegan eggs
- 2 tablespoons water
- 1 ½ breadcrumbs
- 1 zucchini, sliced into wedges
- ½ tablespoon red-wine vinegar
- 2 tablespoons tomato paste
- Salt and pepper to taste

Method:
1. Spray air fryer basket with oil.
2. Put the flour in a dish.
3. In another dish, combine vegan eggs and water.
4. In a third dish, put the breadcrumbs.
5. Dip each zucchini strip into the three dishes, first the flour, then the eggs and water, and lastly the breadcrumbs.
6. Cook in the air fryer at 360 degrees F for 12 minutes, shaking once.
7. Mix the rest of the ingredients in a bowl.
8. Serve zucchini fries with dipping sauce.

Nutritional Value:
- Calories: 235
- Fat: 12 g
- Carbs: 26 g
- Fiber: 2 g
- Protein: 6 g

Sweet Potato Chips

Preparation Time: 40 minutes; Cooking Time: 15 minutes; Servings: 4

Ingredients:

- 1 sweet potato, sliced into thin rounds
- 1 bowl water
- 1 tablespoon olive oil
- Salt and pepper to taste
- Cooking spray

Method:

1. Soak sweet potato slices in a bowl of water for 30 minutes.
2. Drain and then dry with paper towels.
3. Toss in oil and season with salt and pepper.
4. Spray air fryer basket with oil.
5. Cook sweet potato at 350 degrees F for 15 minutes, shaking every 5 minutes.

Nutritional Value:

- Calories: 62
- Fat: 4 g
- Carbs: 14 g
- Fiber: 1 g
- Protein: 0 g

Garlic Mushrooms

Preparation Time: 10 minutes; Cooking Time: 15 minutes; Servings: 2

Ingredients:

- 8 oz. mushrooms, rinsed, dried and sliced in half
- 1 tablespoon olive oil
- ½ teaspoon garlic powder
- Salt and pepper to taste
- 1 teaspoon Worcestershire sauce
- 1 tablespoon parsley, chopped

Method:

1. Toss mushrooms in oil.
2. Season with garlic powder, salt, pepper and Worcestershire sauce.
3. Cook at 380 degrees F for 10 minutes, shaking halfway through.
4. Top with parsley before serving.

Nutritional Value:

- Calories: 90
- Fat: 7.4g
- Carbs: 4.9g
- Fiber: 1.3g
- Protein: 3.8g

Chapter 8: Salad Recipes

Roasted Butternut Squash Salad

Preparation Time: 10 minutes; Cooking Time: 15 minutes; Servings: 4

Ingredients:
- 1 small shallot, peeled, minced
- 1 small butternut squash, peeled, deseeded, 1-inch cubed
- 1 small apple, cored, sliced
- 6 ounces arugula
- 1/4 teaspoon salt
- 1/4 teaspoon cayenne pepper
- 1 teaspoon all-purpose seasoning
- 2 tablespoons lemon juice
- 4 tablespoons olive oil
- 1/2 cup toasted sliced almonds
- 1/2 cup grated vegan Parmesan cheese

Method:
1. Switch on the air fryer, insert the fryer basket, then shut it with the lid, set the frying temperature 400 degrees F, and let it preheat for 5 minutes.
2. Meanwhile, take a large bowl, place squash in it, seasoning with all-purpose seasoning and cayenne pepper, drizzle with 2 tablespoons oil and toss until coated.
3. Open the preheated fryer, place squash in it, close the lid and cook for 15 minutes until golden brown and cooked, shaking halfway.
4. Meanwhile, take a large bowl, place shallots in it, season with salt, drizzle with lemon juice and remaining olive oil, whisk until combined, add arugula and toss until coated.
5. When done, the air fryer will beep and then open the lid and transfer squash to a plate.
6. Assemble the salad and for this, distribute arugula between four plates, top with apples and roasted squash and then sprinkle with cheese and almonds.
7. Chill the salad for 15 minutes in the refrigerator and then serve straight away.

Nutrition Value:
- Calories: 249
- Fat: 13 g
- Carbs: 35 g
- Protein: 5 g
- Fiber: 6.2 g

Garlic and Lemon Mushroom Salad

Preparation Time: 5 minutes; Cooking Time: 10 minutes; Servings: 2

Ingredients:
- 8 ounces mushrooms
- 1/2 teaspoon garlic powder
- 1 tablespoon chopped parsley
- 1 teaspoon soy sauce
- ½ teaspoon salt
- 1/3 teaspoon ground black pepper
- 2 tablespoons olive oil
- 2 wedges of lemon for serving

Method:
1. Switch on the air fryer, insert the fryer basket, then shut it with the lid, set the frying temperature 380 degrees F, and let it preheat for 5 minutes.
2. Meanwhile, cut mushrooms in quarters, then place them in a bowl, add remaining ingredients, except for lemon wedges and toss until coated.
3. Open the preheated fryer, place mushrooms in it, close the lid and cook for 10 minutes until golden brown and cooked, shaking halfway.
4. When done, the air fryer will beep, open the lid, and transfer mushrooms to the salad bowls.
5. Let mushroom cool for 10 minutes and then serve straight away.

Nutrition Value:
- Calories: 110
- Fat: 3 g
- Carbs: 15 g
- Protein: 2 g
- Fiber: 2 g

Taco Salad Bowl

Preparation Time: 10 minutes; Cooking Time: 7 minutes; Servings: 4

Ingredients:
- 1 flour tortilla, burrito size
- Olive oil spray
- Taco filling as needed

Method:
1. Switch on the air fryer, then shut it with the lid, set the frying temperature 400 degrees F, and let it preheat for 5 minutes.
2. Meanwhile, spray tortilla with oil on both sides, then double over with a large piece of foil on both sides; it should be slightly larger than a tortilla, press it into the fryer basket and shape it into a bowl by placing ramekins in the middle.
3. Open the preheated fryer, insert the fryer basket, close the lid and cook for 5 minutes, then remove the ramekin and foil and continue cooking for 2 minutes until the edges of the tortilla are golden brown.
4. When done, the air fryer will beep, open the lid, and lift out the taco bowl.
5. Let it cool for 10 minutes, then fill it with favorite stuffing and serve.

Nutrition Value:
- Calories: 82
- Fat: 4 g
- Carbs: 9 g
- Protein: 1 g
- Fiber: 2 g

Sweet Potato Croutons Salad

Preparation Time: 5 minutes; Cooking Time: 20 minutes; Servings: 4

Ingredients:
- 12s-ounce baked sweet potato, skin-on, cut into pieces
- 2 mandarin oranges, peeled, segmented, halved
- 1-pound mixed salad greens and vegetables
- 1 sweet apple, cored, diced, air fried
- 2 tablespoons balsamic vinegar
- 1/3 cup pomegranate seeds

Method:
1. Switch on the air fryer, insert the fryer basket, then shut it with the lid, set the frying temperature 350 degrees F, and let it preheat for 5 minutes.
2. Meanwhile, prepare sweet potatoes, and for this, dice them into small pieces.
3. Open the preheated fryer, place sweet potatoes in it in a single layer, spray with olive oil, close the lid and cook for 20 minutes until golden brown and cooked, shaking halfway.
4. When done, the air fryer will beep, open the lid, and then transfer sweet potato croutons to a salad bowl.
5. Add remaining ingredients, gently stir until combined, and then serve.

Nutrition Value:
- Calories: 205
- Fat: 14 g
- Carbs: 15 g
- Protein: 5 g
- Fiber: 2 g

Brussel sprouts Salad

Preparation Time: 5 minutes; Cooking Time: 9 minutes; Servings: 2

Ingredients:
- 12 Brussel sprouts, cored, leaves removed
- 1 ½ tablespoons capers
- 2 tablespoons toasted sliced almonds
- 2 teaspoons chopped parsley
- 1/8 teaspoon ground black pepper
- 1/8 teaspoon red chili flakes
- 1/8 teaspoon salt
- 1 ½ tablespoon red wine vinegar
- 2 teaspoons and 1 ½ tablespoon olive oil

Method:
1. Switch on the air fryer, insert the fryer basket, then shut it with the lid, set the frying temperature 400 degrees F, and let it preheat for 5 minutes.
2. Meanwhile, take a large bowl, place sprouts in it, add 1 ½ tablespoon olive oil and toss until coated.
3. Open the preheated fryer, place sprouts in it in, close the lid and cook for 9 minutes until golden brown and cooked, shaking halfway.
4. When done, the air fryer will beep, open the lid, and transfer sprouts to a dish lined with paper towels to remove excess oil.
5. Then remove the paper towels, add remaining ingredients, and toss until combined.
6. Serve straight away.

Nutrition Value:
- Calories: 228
- Fat: 20 g
- Carbs: 11 g
- Protein: 5 g
- Fiber: 5 g

Roasted Vegetable and Pasta Salad

Preparation Time: 10 minutes; Cooking Time: 1 hour and 35 minutes; Servings: 16

Ingredients:
- 4 cups whole-grain pasta, cooked
- 3 small eggplants, destemmed
- 2 medium green bell peppers, deseeded, chopped
- 4 medium tomatoes, cut in eighths
- 3 medium zucchini, trimmed
- 1 cup cherry tomatoes, sliced
- 2 teaspoons salt
- ½ cup Italian dressing
- 2 tablespoons olive oil
- 8 tablespoons grated parmesan cheese
- Olive oil spray

Method:
1. Switch on the air fryer, insert the fryer basket, then shut it with the lid, set the frying temperature 350 degrees F, and let it preheat for 5 minutes.
2. Meanwhile, cut the eggplant into ½-inch thick round slices, place them in a bowl, drizzle with 1 tablespoon oil and toss until coated.
3. Open the preheated fryer, place eggplant pieces in it, close the lid, and cook for 40 minutes until cooked and very tender, shaking halfway.
4. Meanwhile, cut zucchini into ½-inch thick round slices, place them in a bowl, drizzle with 1 tablespoon oil and toss until coated.
5. When done, the air fryer will beep, open the lid and transfer eggplant to a dish.
6. Place zucchini into the fryer basket, close the lid, and cook for 25 minutes until cooked and very tender, shaking halfway.
7. When done, the air fryer will beep, open the lid and transfer zucchini to a dish containing eggplant.
8. Place tomato slices into the fryer basket, spray with olive oil, close the lid and cook for 30 minutes until cooked and very tender, shaking halfway.
9. Then take a large salad bowl, place peppers in it, then add cherry tomatoes and all the roasted vegetables, add remaining ingredients and toss until well mixed.
10. Chill the salad for 20 minutes in the refrigerated and then serve straight away.

Nutrition Value:
- Calories: 121
- Fat: 4 g
- Carbs: 23 g
- Protein: 5 g
- Fiber: 4 g

Crispy Tofu & Avocado Salad

Preparation Time: 15 minutes; Cooking Time: 15 minutes; Servings: 6

Ingredients:

- Cooking spray
- 2 cups tofu, cubed
- 4 cups mixed greens
- 4 cups Romaine lettuce
- ½ cup onion, sliced
- 1 cup cherry tomatoes, sliced in half
- ½ avocado, sliced into cubes
- ½ cup red wine vinegar
- 1 cup avocado lime dressing

Method:

1. Spray air fryer basket with oil.
2. Cook the tofu cubes at 375 degrees F for 15 minutes, shaking halfway through.
3. In a bowl, arrange the salad by topping the lettuce and mixed greens with crispy tofu, onion, tomatoes and avocado.
4. Drizzle with red wine vinegar and avocado lime dressing.

Nutritional Value:

- Calories: 287
- Fat: 10.8g
- Carbs: 33.1g
- Fiber: 12g
- Protein: 16.8g

Vegetable & Pasta Salad

Preparation Time: 1 hour and 5 minutes; Cooking Time: 1 hour and 45 minutes; Servings: 4

Ingredients:

- 3 eggplants, sliced
- 2 tablespoons olive oil, divided
- Salt and pepper to taste
- 3 zucchinis, sliced
- 4 tomatoes, sliced into wedges
- 4 cups macaroni pasta
- Salt to taste
- 8 tablespoons vegan Parmesan cheese, grated
- ½ cup Italian dressing
- Basil leaves, chopped

Method:

1. Toss eggplant slices in 1 tablespoon olive oil and season with salt and pepper.
2. Cook in the air fryer at 375 degrees F for 40 minutes.
3. Toss the zucchini in the remaining oil and cook in the air fryer for 25 minutes.
4. Cook pasta according to the package directions. Drain and rinse.
5. Toss the pasta with the eggplant and zucchini slices.
6. Drizzle with Italian dressing.
7. Season with salt.
8. Sprinkle cheese and basil on top, and serve.

Nutritional Value:

- Calories: 336
- Fat: 11.7g
- Carbs: 52g
- Fiber: 13.1g
- Protein: 9.3g

Rainbow Vegetables Salad

Preparation Time: 5 minutes; Cooking Time: 20 minutes; Servings: 4

Ingredients:
- 1 medium red bell pepper, deseeded, diced
- 1/2 of medium sweet onion, cut into wedges
- 1 medium yellow summer squash, diced
- 1 zucchini, diced
- 4 ounces mushrooms, halved
- 1/3 teaspoon ground black pepper
- 2/3 teaspoon salt
- 1 tablespoon olive oil

Method:
1. Switch on the air fryer, insert the fryer basket, then shut it with the lid, set the frying temperature 350 degrees F, and let it preheat for 5 minutes.
2. Meanwhile, take a large bowl, place all the vegetables in it, drizzle with oil, season with salt and black pepper and toss until coated.
3. Open the preheated fryer, place vegetables in it, close the lid and cook for 20 minutes until golden brown and cooked, shaking halfway.
4. When done, the air fryer will beep, open the lid and transfer vegetables to a dish.
5. Serve straight away.

Nutrition Value:
- Calories: 69
- Fat: 3.8 g
- Carbs: 7.7 g
- Protein: 2.6 g
- Fiber: 2.3 g

Salad Topped with Garlic Croutons

Preparation Time: 10 minutes; Cooking Time: 5 minutes; Servings: 4

Ingredients:

- 4 slices vegan bread, sliced into cubes
- 1 tablespoon olive oil
- Garlic powder to taste
- Salt and pepper to taste
- 1 teaspoon Italian seasoning
- Mixed greens
- 1 cup tomato, chopped
- 1 cup white onion rings

Method:

1. Coat the bread cubes with olive oil.
2. Season with garlic powder, salt, pepper and Italian seasoning.
3. Cook in the air fryer at 380 degrees F for 5 minutes, shaking a few times.
4. Place the mixed greens in a bowl,
5. Top with the tomato, white onions and croutons.
6. Serve with vegan salad dressing.

Nutritional Value:

- Calories: 50
- Fat: 4.1g
- Carbs: 4g
- Fiber: 0.6g
- Protein: 0.4g

Green Bean Salad

Preparation Time: 35 minutes; Cooking Time: 15 minutes; Servings: 2

Ingredients:

- 2 cups green beans, trimmed
- ¼ cup water
- ¼ cup vegan mayo
- ¼ cup vegan cheese

Method:

1. Put the green beans and water in a small heatproof pan.
2. Put the pan in the air fryer basket.
3. Cook in the air fryer at 375 degrees F for 15 minutes.
4. Let cool.
5. Put in the refrigerator for 30 minutes.
6. Mix with mayo and top with cheese.

Nutritional Value:

- Calories: 97
- Fat: 6.1g
- Carbs: 10.1g
- Fiber: 3.9g
- Protein: 2g

Italian Tofu Salad

Preparation Time: 5 minutes; Cooking Time: 10 minutes; Servings: 2

Ingredients:

- 8 ounces tofu, extra-firm, pressed, drained
- 1/2 teaspoon dried oregano
- 1/4 teaspoon onion powder
- 1/2 teaspoon garlic powder
- 1/2 teaspoon dried basil
- ¼ teaspoon ground black pepper
- 1 tablespoon soy sauce
- 1 tablespoon chickpeas liquid

Method:

1. Switch on the air fryer, insert the fryer basket, then shut it with the lid, set the frying temperature 350 degrees F, and let it preheat for 5 minutes.
2. Meanwhile, paper tofu and for this, cut tofu into ten cubed, place them in a plastic bag, add remaining ingredients, seal the bag and shake well until coated.
3. Open the preheated fryer, place tofu in it in a single layer, close the lid and cook for 10 minutes until golden brown and cooked, turning halfway.
4. When done, the air fryer will beep and then open the lid and transfer tofu to a salad bowl.
5. Serve straight away.

Nutrition Value:

- Calories: 87
- Fat: 4.4 g
- Carbs: 3.4 g
- Protein: 10 g
- Fiber: 1.3 g

Salad with Roasted Tomatoes

Preparation Time: 5 minutes; Cooking Time: 45 minutes; Servings: 4

Ingredients:

- 2 cups tomatoes, sliced
- Salt to taste
- 4 cups Romaine lettuce leaves
- 2 cups arugula
- 1 cup onion, chopped
- Vegan salad dressing

Method:

1. Toss tomato slices in olive oil.
2. Season with salt.
3. Cook in the air fryer at 240 degrees F for 45 minutes.
4. Arrange lettuce and arugula on salad bowls.
5. Top with onion and roasted tomatoes.
6. Serve with vegan salad dressing.

Nutritional Value:

- Calories: 73
- Fat: 3.9g
- Carbs: 8.7g
- Fiber: 2.2g
- Protein: 1.6g

Vegetable Salad with Chimichurri Vinaigrette

Preparation Time: 5 minutes; Cooking Time: 30 minutes; Servings: 4

Ingredients:

For the Salad:
- 1/2 head of medium purple cauliflower, cut into small florets
- 2 cups baby arugula
- 3 small red beets, peeled, 1/4-inch thick diced
- 1/2 head of medium white cauliflower, cut into small florets
- 1 medium head of frisee, torn into small pieces
- 1/2 head of medium yellow cauliflower, cut into small florets
- 6 breakfast radishes, peeled, sliced
- 1 1/3 teaspoon salt
- ¾ teaspoon ground black pepper
- 1 small bunch of mint, slivered
- Olive oil spray

For the Vinaigrette:
- 1 clove of garlic, peeled
- 1/2 bunch of chives, chopped
- 1 lemon, juiced
- 1 bunch of cilantro, leaves chopped
- 1 medium shallot, peeled, chopped
- 1 bunch parsley, leaves chopped
- 1/3 teaspoon ground black pepper
- 1/8 teaspoon red pepper flakes
- 2/3 teaspoon salt
- 1/2 cup olive oil
- 1/4 cup red wine vinegar

Method:
1. Switch on the air fryer, insert the fryer basket, then shut it with the lid, set the frying temperature 360 degrees F, and let it preheat for 5 minutes.
2. Meanwhile, place white, yellow, and purple cauliflower in separate large bowls, place beets in another bowl, then season all the cauliflower and beets with salt and black pepper, drizzle with oil and toss until well coated.
3. Open the preheated fryer, place seasoned white cauliflower in it in a single layer, close the lid and cook for 8 minutes until golden brown and cooked, shaking halfway.
4. When done, the air fryer will beep, open the lid, transfer florets to a dish and then cook yellow cauliflower and purple cauliflower separately in the same manner.

5. When cauliflowers have roasted, add beets into the fryer basket in a single layer, close the lid and cook for 14 minutes until golden brown and cooked, shaking halfway.
6. Meanwhile, prepare the vinaigrette and for this, place all of its ingredients in a food processor, except for oil, pulse for 1 minute and then slowly blend in oil until smooth.
7. Assemble the salad and for this, place all the roasted vegetables in a large bowl, pour in vinaigrette, and toss until well coated.
8. Then add remaining vegetables, toss until mixed, garnish with mint and serve.

Nutrition Value:
- Calories: 434
- Fat: 19.1 g
- Carbs: 59.5 g
- Protein: 11.5 g
- Fiber: 12.5 g

Fried Chickpea Salad

Preparation Time: 5 minutes; Cooking Time: 10 minutes; Servings: 4

Ingredients:
- 1 1/2 cups cooked chickpeas
- 1/2 teaspoon onion powder
- 1/8 teaspoon salt
- 2 teaspoons nutritional yeast
- Olive oil spray

For the Salad:
- ¼ cup chopped green onion
- ¼ cup chopped tomatoes
- 2 tablespoons chopped green chilies

Method:
1. Switch on the air fryer, insert the fryer basket, then shut it with the lid, set the frying temperature 400 degrees F, and let it preheat for 5 minutes.
2. Meanwhile, take a bowl, add chickpeas in it, spray generously with oil, add onion, salt and yeast and toss until mixed.
3. Open the preheated fryer, place chickpeas in it, close the lid and cook for 7 minutes until golden brown and cooked, shaking halfway.
4. When done, the air fryer will beep, then open the lid and transfer chickpeas to a salad bowl.
5. Cool chickpeas for 10 minutes, then add all the ingredients for the salad in it and toss until mixed.
6. Serve straight away.

Nutrition Value:
- Calories: 105
- Fat: 1 g
- Carbs: 17 g
- Protein: 5 g
- Fiber: 4 g

Radish & Mozzarella Salad

Preparation Time: 15 minutes; Cooking Time: 30 minutes; Servings: 4

Ingredients:

- 1 lb. radish, sliced into rounds
- 2 tablespoons olive oil
- Salt and pepper to taste
- ½ lb. vegan mozzarella, sliced into rounds
- 2 tablespoons balsamic glaze

Method:

1. Toss radish rounds in oil and season with salt and pepper.
2. Cook in the air fryer at 350 degrees F for 30 minutes, shaking once or twice during cooking.
3. Arrange on a serving platter with the vegan mozzarella.
4. Drizzle cheese and radish with balsamic glaze before serving.

Nutritional Value:

- Calories: 88
- Fat: 7.7g
- Carbs: 4g
- Fiber: 1.8g
- Protein: 1.8g

Mixed Greens with Corn

Preparation Time: 15 minutes; Cooking Time: 10 minutes; Servings: 2

Ingredients:

- 3 ears corn
- Cooking spray
- Salt and pepper to taste
- 3 cups mixed greens
- 1 cup cucumber, sliced into small cubes
- 1 cup tomatoes, chopped
- Vegan salad dressing

Method:

1. Preheat your air fryer to 400 degrees F.
2. Spray corn with oil.
3. Season with salt and pepper.
4. Cook in the air fryer for 10 minutes, flipping halfway through.
5. Remove from heat and slice to get the kernels.
6. Put mixed greens in salad bowls.
7. Top with cucumber, tomatoes and corn kernels.
8. Serve with the dressing.

Nutritional Value:

- Calories: 157
- Fat: 3.5g
- Carbs: 28.6g
- Fiber: 6.6g
- Protein: 5.5g

Roasted Vegetable Salad

Preparation Time: 1 hour and 30 minutes; Cooking Time: 25 minutes; Servings: 6

Ingredients:

- 1 sweet potato, chopped
- 1 red bell pepper, chopped
- 1 onion, chopped
- 4 small potatoes, chopped
- ¼ cup cherry tomatoes, chopped
- Salt and pepper to taste
- ¼ cup parsley, chopped
- 2 tablespoons capers, chopped
- 1 avocado, chopped
- 1 tablespoon lemon juice
- 1 tablespoon olive oil
- 1 can chickpeas mixed with 1 teaspoon mustard powder
- 4 cups lettuce leaves, chopped

Method:

1. Season all the vegetables (except parsley, capers, lettuce and avocado) with salt and pepper.
2. Toss in oil and cook in the air fryer at 400 degrees for 25 minutes.
3. Transfer to a bowl and refrigerate for 1 hour.
4. Mash avocado and mix with lemon juice and olive oil.
5. Arrange the salad in a bowl by putting the lettuce leaves first and topping with the cooked vegetables and chickpeas.
6. Serve with the avocado dressing.

Nutritional Value:

- Calories: 206
- Fat: 9.2g
- Carbs: 29.6g
- Fiber: 6.8g
- Protein: 3.7g

Roasted Butternut Squash Salad

Preparation Time: 10 minutes; Cooking Time: 15 minutes; Servings: 4

Ingredients:

- 1 butternut squash, sliced into cubes
- 4 tablespoons olive oil, divided
- ¼ teaspoon cayenne pepper
- Salt to taste
- 2 tablespoons fresh lemon juice
- 1 shallot, minced
- 6 oz. arugula
- 1 apple, sliced thinly
- ½ cup almonds, toasted and sliced
- ½ cup vegan Parmesan cheese, grated

Method:

1. Toss squash cubes in 1 tablespoon olive oil and cayenne pepper.
2. Add to the air fryer and cook at 400 degrees F for 15 minutes, shaking once or twice.
3. In a bowl, mix the salt, remaining olive oil, lemon juice and shallot.
4. Coat arugula with this mixture.
5. Arrange arugula on salad bowls.
6. Top with the squash cubes, apple slices, almonds and Parmesan cheese.

Nutritional Value:

- Calories: 295
- Fat: 20.5g
- Carbs: 28.8g
- Fiber: 6.4g
- Protein: 5.3g

Green Salad with Roasted Bell Peppers

Preparation Time: 10 minutes; Cooking Time: 10 minutes; Servings: 4

Ingredients:

- 1 red bell pepper
- 1 tablespoon lemon juice
- 2 tablespoons olive oil
- 3 tablespoons vegan yogurt
- Pepper to taste
- 4 cups Romaine lettuce, chopped

Method:

1. Preheat your air fryer to 400 degrees F.
2. Add the bell pepper inside.
3. Cook for 10 minutes or until slightly charred.
4. Slice the roasted bell peppers.
5. Top the Romaine lettuce with the roasted bell peppers.
6. In a bowl, mix the rest of the ingredients and serve as dressing.

Nutritional Value:

- Calories: 205
- Fat: 14g
- Carbs: 18.3g
- Fiber: 0.8g
- Protein: 3.6g

Chapter 9: Dessert Recipes

Carrot Cake

Preparation Time: 10 minutes; Cooking Time: 15 minutes; Serving: 1

Ingredients:

- Cooking spray
- ¼ cups whole wheat pastry flour
- ¼ teaspoon baking powder
- 1 tablespoon coconut sugar
- 1/8 teaspoon ground dried ginger
- ¼ teaspoon ground cinnamon
- Salt to taste
- 2 tablespoons almond milk
- 2 teaspoons oil
- 2 tablespoons carrot, grated
- 1 tablespoons date, chopped
- 2 tablespoons walnuts, chopped
- Water

Method:

1. Spray a heatproof mug with oil.
2. In a bowl, mix the flour, baking powder, sugar, ginger, cinnamon and salt.
3. Pour in the milk and oil.
4. Add the carrot, dates and walnuts.
5. Mix well.
6. Put the mug inside the air fryer.
7. Pour water around it.
8. Cook in the air fryer at 350 degrees for 15 minutes or until middle part is fully cooked.

Nutritional Value:

- Calories: 365
- Fat: 17.5g
- Carbs: 48g
- Fiber: 6.3g
- Protein: 7.8g

Donuts

Preparation Time: 5 minutes; Cooking Time: 18 minutes; Servings: 2

Ingredients:
- 3 cups cherries, pitted, halved
- 1/2 teaspoon almond extract, unsweetened
- 2 tablespoons maple syrup
- 4 tablespoons granola
- 1 tablespoon almond butter melted

Method:
1. Switch on the air fryer, insert the fryer basket, then shut it with the lid, set the frying temperature 350 degrees F, and let it preheat for 5 minutes.
2. Meanwhile, take a large ramekin, place cherries in it, and then stir in almond extract, butter and maple syrup until mixed.
3. Open the preheated fryer, place ramekin in it, close the lid and cook for 15 minutes until cooked, stirring halfway.
4. When done, the air fryer will beep, open the lid, top cherries with granola, and then continue cooking for 3 minutes until the top has turned brown.
5. Serve straight away.

Nutrition Value:
- Calories: 316
- Fat: 7 g
- Carbs: 62 g
- Protein: 4 g
- Fiber: 6 g

Cinnamon Churros

Preparation Time: 60 minutes; Cooking Time: 25 minutes; Servings: 4

Ingredients:

For the Churros:
- 1 cup coconut flour
- 1/2 cup and 1 tablespoon coconut sugar
- 2 teaspoons cinnamon
- 1/2 teaspoon vanilla extract, unsweetened
- 1/2 cup almond butter
- 3 flax eggs
- 1 cup of water

For the Chocolate Sauce:
- 1 teaspoon coconut oil
- 3/4 cup chocolate chips, unsweetened

Method:
1. Prepare churros and for this, take a medium saucepan, place it over medium heat, pour in water and bring it to a boil.
2. Stir in butter and 1 tablespoon sugar, let it melts, switch heat to medium-low level and then fold in the flour until incorporated and the dough comes together, remove the pan from heat and set aside until required.
3. Take a medium bowl, place flax eggs in it and whisk in vanilla until combined.
4. Fold the flax egg mixture into the prepared dough until well combined and then let it stand for 15 minutes until cooked.
5. Transfer cooled dough into a piping bag with a star-shaped tip, take a baking pan, line it with parchment paper and pipe churros on it, about 6-inch long, and then chill them in the refrigerator for 30 minutes.
6. Meanwhile, switch on the air fryer, insert the fryer basket, then shut it with the lid, set the frying temperature 380 degrees F, and let it preheat.
7. Then open the preheated fryer, place churros in it in a single layer, close the lid and cook for 10 minutes until golden brown and cooked, shaking halfway.
8. Meanwhile, take a small bowl, place the cinnamon and remaining sugar in it and stir until mixed, set aside until required.
9. When done, the air fryer will beep, then open the lid, dredge churros into the cinnamon-sugar mixture, place them on a wire rack and cook remaining churros in the same manner.

10. In the meantime, prepare the chocolate sauce and for this, take a heatproof bowl, place chocolate chips in it, add oil and microwave for 30 seconds until chocolate has melted, and when done, stir well.
11. Dip churros into the chocolate sauce and serve.

Nutrition Value:
- Calories: 290
- Fat: 15 g
- Carbs: 37 g
- Protein: 3 g
- Fiber: 2 g

Apple and Blueberries Crumble

Preparation Time: 5 minutes; Cooking Time: 15 minutes; Servings: 2

Ingredients:
- 1/2 cup frozen blueberries
- 1 medium apple, peeled, diced
- 2 tablespoons coconut sugar
- 1/4 cup and 1 tablespoon brown rice flour
- 1/2 teaspoon ground cinnamon
- 2 tablespoons almond butter

Method:
1. Switch on the air fryer, insert the fryer basket, then shut it with the lid, set the frying temperature 350 degrees F, and let it preheat for 5 minutes.
2. Meanwhile, take a large ramekin, place apples and berries in it, and stir until mixed.
3. Take a small bowl, add flour and remaining ingredients in it, stir until mixed, and then spoon this mixture over fruits.
4. Open the preheated fryer, place the prepared ramekin in it in, close the lid and cook for 15 minutes until cooked and the top has turned golden brown.
5. When done, the air fryer will beep, then open the lid and remove ramekin from it.
6. Serve straight away.

Nutrition Value:
- Calories: 310
- Fat: 12 g
- Carbs: 50 g
- Protein: 2 g
- Fiber: 5 g

Baked Apples

Preparation Time: 5 minutes; Cooking Time: 11 minutes; Servings: 4

Ingredients:
- 2 medium apples, cored
- 2 tablespoons coconut sugar
- 2/3 teaspoon ground cinnamon

Method:
1. Switch on the air fryer, insert the fryer basket, then shut it with the lid, set the frying temperature 360 degrees F, and let it preheat for 5 minutes.
2. Meanwhile, prepare the apples and for this, slice each apple lengthwise, and then remove the seeds.
3. Open the preheated fryer, place apples in it in a single layer, close the lid and cook for 10 minutes until tender.
4. Meanwhile, take a small bowl, stir together sugar and cinnamon in it, and set aside until required.
5. When done, the air fryer will beep, then open the lid, sprinkle sugar-cinnamon mixture on apples, shut with lid, and continue cooking for 1 minute.
6. When done, transfer apples to a dish and then serve.

Nutrition Value:
- Calories: 81
- Fat: 0 g
- Carbs: 22 g
- Protein: 0 g
- Fiber: 5 g

Stuffed and Spiced Baked Apples

Preparation Time: 5 minutes; Cooking Time: 10 minutes; Servings: 4

Ingredients:
- 1/3 cup rolled oats
- 4 medium apples
- 1/4 cup chopped pecans
- 1 teaspoon pumpkin spice seasoning
- 2 tablespoons raisins
- 1/4 cup maple syrup
- 2/3 cup water

Method:
1. Switch on the air fryer, insert the fryer basket, then shut it with the lid, set the frying temperature 340 degrees F, and let it preheat for 5 minutes.
2. Meanwhile, prepare the apples and for this, core them from the center but not all the way through the bottom and scoop out the seeds by using a spoon.
3. Take a medium bowl, place remaining ingredients in it, except for water, stir until mixed and stuff this mixture into the apples.
4. Take a shallow heatproof dish that fits into the air fryer, pour water in it, and place prepared apples in it.
5. Open the preheated fryer, place the dish containing apples in it, close the lid and cook for 15 minutes until fork-tender, turning and spraying with oil halfway.
6. When done, the air fryer will beep, then open the lid and take out the dish.
7. Serve straight away.

Nutrition Value:
- Calories: 178.4
- Fat: 4.3 g
- Carbs: 44.3 g
- Protein: 0.7 g
- Fiber: 4.9 g

Vegan Brownies

Preparation Time: 15 minutes; Cooking Time: 20 minutes; Servings: 4

Ingredients:
- ½ cup whole wheat pastry flour
- ¼ cup cocoa powder
- ½ cup sugar
- 1 tablespoon ground flax seeds
- ¼ teaspoon salt
- ¼ cup almond milk
- ¼ cup aquafaba
- ½ teaspoon vanilla extract
- Chopped walnuts
- Cooking spray

Method:
1. Combine first five ingredients in a bowl.
2. Mix the rest of the ingredients except the walnuts in another bowl.
3. Slowly combine the two bowls.
4. Preheat your air fryer to 350 degrees F.
5. Spray air fryer with oil.
6. Pour the mixture into a heatproof pan.
7. Sprinkle top with walnuts.
8. Cook in the air fryer for 20 minutes.

Nutritional Value:
- Calories: 206
- Fat: 5.1g
- Carbs: 40.4g
- Fiber: 3.9g
- Protein: 3.1g

Roasted Bananas

Preparation Time: 5 minutes; Cooking Time: 5 minutes; Servings: 2

Ingredients:

- 2 cups bananas, cubed
- 1 teaspoon avocado oil
- 1 tablespoon maple syrup
- 1 teaspoon brown sugar
- 1 cup almond milk

Method:

1. Coat the banana cubes with oil and maple syrup.
2. Sprinkle with brown sugar.
3. Cook in the air fryer at 375 degrees F for 5 minutes.
4. Drizzle milk on top of the bananas before serving.

Nutritional Value:

- Calories: 107
- Fat: 0.7g
- Carbs: 27g
- Fiber: 3.1g
- Protein: 1.3g
- Sugars 14g

Fruit Kebab

Preparation Time: 30 minutes; Cooking Time: 6 minutes; Servings: 10

Ingredients:

- 1 teaspoon maple syrup
- 1 teaspoon lemon juice
- 1 apple, diced
- 1 mango, diced
- 1 pear, diced
- Salt to taste
- Lemon zest

Method:

1. In a bowl, combine maple syrup and lemon juice.
2. Coat the fruit cubes with the mixture.
3. Season with salt.
4. Arrange in skewers.
5. Place the skewers inside the air fryer and cook at 360 degrees for 5 minutes.
6. Garnish with lemon zest.

Nutritional Value:

- Calories: 52
- Fat: 0.2g
- Carbs: 13.4g
- Fiber: 1.9g
- Protein: 0.5g

Pear Crisp

Preparation Time: 10 minutes; Cooking Time: 25 minutes; Servings: 2

Ingredients:

- 1 cup flour
- 1 stick vegan butter
- 1 tablespoon cinnamon
- ½ cup sugar
- 2 pears, cubed

Method:

1. Mix flour and butter to form crumbly texture.
2. Add cinnamon and sugar.
3. Put the pears in the air fryer.
4. Pour and spread the mixture on top of the pears.
5. Cook at 350 degrees F for 25 minutes.

Nutritional Value:

- Calories: 544
- Fat: 0.9g
- Carbs: 132.3g
- Fiber: 10g
- Protein: 7.4g

Sweetened Plantains

Preparation Time: 5 minutes; Cooking Time: 8 minutes; Servings: 4

Ingredients:

- 2 ripe plantains, sliced
- 2 teaspoons avocado oil
- Salt to taste
- Maple syrup

Method:

1. Toss the plantains in oil.
2. Season with salt.
3. Cook in the air fryer basket at 400 degrees F for 10 minutes, shaking after 5 minutes.
4. Drizzle with maple syrup before serving.

Nutritional Value:

- Calories: 125
- Fat: 0.6g
- Carbs: 32g
- Fiber: 2.2g
- Protein: 1.2g

Peanut Butter Balls

Preparation Time: 15 minutes; Cooking Time: 20 minutes; Servings: 6

Ingredients:
- 1/2 cup coconut flour
- 2 tablespoons flaxseed
- 1/2 cup oats
- 1/2 teaspoon baking soda
- 1/3 cup maple syrup
- 1/2 teaspoon baking powder
- 1/2 cup peanut butter
- 5 tablespoons water, warmed

Method:
1. Prepare the flax egg and for this, place flax seeds a small bowl, stir in water until combined and let it stand for 5 minutes.
2. Then pour flax egg in a large bowl, add butter and maple syrup, whisk until smooth and then whisk in baking powder and soda until well combined.
3. Stir in oats and flour until incorporated and dough comes together, place the dough into the refrigerator for 10 minutes until chilled, and then shape the dough into twelve balls.
4. Meanwhile, switch on the air fryer, insert the fryer basket, then shut it with the lid, set the frying temperature 250 degrees F, and let it preheat for 5 minutes.
5. Open the preheated fryer, place balls in it in a single layer, close the lid and cook for 10 minutes until golden brown and cooked, shaking halfway.
6. When done, the air fryer will beep, then open the lid, and transfer balls to a dish.
7. Cook remaining balls in the same manner and then serve.

Nutrition Value:
- Calories: 97.8
- Fat: 5.5 g
- Carbs: 8.8 g
- Protein: 2.9 g
- Fiber: 1 g

Brownies

Preparation Time: 5 minutes; Cooking Time: 20 minutes; Servings: 4

Ingredients:

The Wet Ingredients:
- 1/4 cup almond milk
- 1/4 cup chickpeas liquid
- 1/2 teaspoon vanilla extract, unsweetened

The Dry Ingredients:
- 1/2 cup whole-wheat pastry flour
- 1/2 cup coconut sugar
- 1/4 cup cocoa powder, unsweetened
- 1 tablespoon ground flax seeds
- 1/4 teaspoon salt

For the Mix-Ins:
- 2 tablespoons chopped walnuts
- 2 tablespoons pecans
- 2 tablespoons shredded coconut

Method:
1. Switch on the air fryer, insert the fryer basket, then shut it with the lid, set the frying temperature 350 degrees F, and let it preheat for 5 minutes.
2. Meanwhile, take a large bowl, add all the dry ingredients in it and stir until mixed.
3. Take another bowl, place all the wet ingredients in it, whisk until combined, then gradually mix into the dry ingredients mixture until incorporated and mix the walnuts, pecans and coconut until combined.
4. Take a 5-inch round pan, line it with parchment paper, pour in prepared batter, smooth the top with a spatula.
5. Open the preheated fryer, place the prepared pan in it, close the lid and cook for 20 minutes until firm and a toothpick come out clean from the center of the pan.
6. When done, the air fryer will beep, then open the lid, remove the pan from the fryer and cool for 15 minutes.
7. Then cut into brownies and serve.

Nutrition Value:
- Calories: 262
- Fat: 9.9 g
- Carbs: 47.9 g
- Protein: 3.2 g
- Fiber: 4.8 g

Apple Chips

Preparation Time: 10 minutes; Cooking Time: 20 minutes; Servings: 2

Ingredients:

- 1 apple, sliced thinly
- Salt to taste
- ¼ teaspoon ground cinnamon

Method:

1. Preheat the air fryer to 350 degrees F.
2. Toss the apple slices in salt and cinnamon.
3. Add to the air fryer.
4. Let cool before serving.

Nutritional Value:

- Calories: 59
- Fat 0.2g
- Carbs: 15.6g
- Fiber: 2.9g
- Protein: 0.3g

Sweet Potato Dessert Fries

Preparation Time: 5 minutes; Cooking Time: 27 minutes; Servings: 2

Ingredients:
- 2 medium sweet potatoes, peeled
- 1/4 cup coconut sugar
- 1 tablespoon cornstarch
- 2 tablespoons cinnamon
- ½ tablespoon coconut oil
- Powdered sugar as needed for dusting

Method:
1. Switch on the air fryer, insert the fryer basket, then shut it with the lid, set the frying temperature 370 degrees F, and let it preheat for 5 minutes.
2. Meanwhile, cut peeled potatoes into ½-inch thick slices, place them in a bowl, add cornstarch and oil and toss until well coated.
3. Open the preheated fryer, place sweet potatoes in it in a single layer, close the lid, and cook for 18 minutes until golden brown and cooked, shaking halfway.
4. When all the fries have cooked, transfer them to a large bowl, sprinkle them with remaining coconut sugar and cinnamon and toss until coated.
5. Transfer potatoes to a dish, sprinkle with powdered sugar, and then serve.

Nutrition Value:
- Calories: 102.6
- Fat: 0.2 g
- Carbs: 23.6 g
- Protein: 2.3 g
- Fiber: 3.8 g

Mug Carrot Cake

Preparation Time: 5 minutes; Cooking Time: 15 minutes; Servings: 1

Ingredients:
- 2 tablespoons grated carrot
- 1/4 cups whole-wheat pastry flour
- 1/8 teaspoon ground dried ginger
- 2 tablespoons chopped walnuts
- 1/4 teaspoon baking powder
- 1 tablespoon coconut sugar
- 1/8 teaspoon salt
- 1/4 teaspoon ground cinnamon
- 1 tablespoons raisin
- 1/8 teaspoon ground allspice
- 2 tablespoons and 2 teaspoons almond milk
- 2 teaspoons olive oil

Method:
1. Switch on the air fryer, insert the fryer basket, then shut it with the lid, set the frying temperature 350 degrees F, and let it preheat for 5 minutes.
2. Meanwhile, take an ovenproof mug, place flour in it, stir in ginger, baking powder, salt, sugar, cinnamon, and allspice until mixed and then mix in carrots, raisins, nuts, oil, and milk until incorporated
3. Open the preheated fryer, place the prepared mug in it, close the lid and cook for 15 minutes until firm and a toothpick come out clean from the center of the cake.
4. When done, the air fryer will beep, then open the lid and take out the mug.
5. Serve straight away.

Nutrition Value:
- Calories: 168.6
- Fat: 11.5 g
- Carbs: 8.8 g
- Protein: 7.8 g
- Fiber: 1.5 g

Donut Holes

Preparation Time: 1 hour and 10 minutes; Cooking Time: 12 minutes; Servings: 6

Ingredients:
- 1 cup almond flour
- 1 teaspoon baking powder
- 1/2 teaspoon salt
- 1/4 cup and 2 tablespoons coconut sugar, divided
- 2 1/4 teaspoons cinnamon, divided
- 1 tablespoon melted coconut oil
- 2 tablespoons chickpea liquid
- 1/4 cup soy milk

Method:
1. Take a large bowl, place flour in it, and stir baking powder, salt, ¼ cup sugar, and 2 teaspoons cinnamon in it.
2. Whisk in oil, milk and chickpea liquid until incorporated and the dough comes together and then chill it in the refrigerator for 1 hour.
3. Take a shallow dish, place remaining sugar and cinnamon in it and stir until mixed, set aside until required.
4. Switch on the air fryer, insert the fryer basket lined with parchment paper, then shut it with the lid, set the frying temperature 370 degrees F, and let it preheat for 5 minutes.
5. Meanwhile, remove chilled dough from the refrigerator, distribute it into twelve parts, shape each part into a ball and then dredge it with cinnamon-sugar mixture.
6. Open the preheated fryer, place balls in it in a single layer, spray with olive oil, close the lid and cook for 6 minutes until golden brown and cooked, don't shake.
7. When done, the air fryer will beep, then open the lid, transfer balls to a dish and let them cool completely.
8. Cook remaining donut balls in the same manner and then serve.

Nutrition Value:
- Calories: 190
- Fat: 9 g
- Carbs: 28 g
- Protein: 2 g
- Fiber: 1 g

Fruit Crumble

Preparation Time: 10 minutes; Cooking Time: 15 minutes; Servings: 4

Ingredients:

- 1 apple, diced
- ¼ cup frozen blueberries
- ¼ cup frozen strawberries
- ¼ cup and 1 tablespoon brown rice flour
- 2 tablespoons sugar
- ½ teaspoon ground cinnamon
- 2 tablespoons vegan butter

Method:

1. Preheat your air fryer to 350 degrees F.
2. In a ramekin, combine the apple, blueberries and strawberries.
3. In another bowl, mix the rest of the ingredients.
4. Serve this mixture over the fruit mix.
5. Cook at 350 degrees F for 15 minutes.

Nutritional Value:

- Calories: 310
- Fat: 12 g
- Carbs: 50 g
- Fiber: 5 g
- Protein: 2 g

Baked Apples with Pumpkin Spice

Preparation Time: 10 minutes; Cooking Time: 15 minutes; Servings: 4

Ingredients:

- 4 apples, sliced
- ¼ cup maple syrup
- ¼ cup rolled oats
- ¼ cup pecans, chopped
- 2 tablespoons raisins
- 1 teaspoon pumpkin spice seasoning
- 2/3 cup water

Method:

1. Coat apple slices with maple syrup and mix with oats, pecans and raisins.
2. Season with pumpkin spice.
3. Transfer the mixture into a small heatproof dish that can fit inside the air fryer.
4. In the air fryer, add the water.
5. Put the dish inside.
6. Cook at 340 degrees F for 15 minutes.

Nutritional Value:

- Calories: 206
- Fat: 1.4g
- Carbs: 51.2g
- Fiber: 6.2g
- Protein: 1.5g

Berry Crumble

Preparation Time: 15 minutes; Cooking Time: 12 minutes; Servings: 4

Ingredients:

- ½ cup blackberries
- ½ cup strawberries
- 1 cup blueberries
- ¼ cup flour
- ¼ cup sugar
- 1 teaspoon vanilla
- ½ cup quick oats
- ¼ cup brown sugar
- 1 teaspoon lemon juice
- 3 tablespoons melted butter

Method:

1. In a bowl, combine the berries, lemon juice and sugar.
2. In another bowl, mix the rest of the ingredients.
3. Toss the berries in the mixture.
4. Spray air fryer with oil.
5. Cook at 390 degrees F for 12 minutes.

Nutritional Value:

- Calories: 262
- Fat: 9.7g
- Carbs: 42.8g
- Fiber: 3.4g
- Protein: 2.9g

Conclusion

In conclusion, classic and freshly invented, seasonal and year-round - these air fryer recipes embody all the fruits, vegetables, legumes, and grains one can think of. This manual is going to arm you with all the techniques you need to shop and cook vegan as well as reach that extra special awesome crisp no other way of cooking can give you. To elevate your vegan kitchen game and prove that vegan versions of family favourites can be nourishing, let's get started!

www.ingramcontent.com/pod-product-compliance
Lightning Source LLC
Chambersburg PA
CBHW081359070526
44583CB00020B/2598